THE

BEAUTY OF IMMANUEL.

HIS NAME SHALL BE CALLED WONDERFUL.

BY

LE ROY J. HALSEY, D. D.

AUTHOR OF "LIFE PICTURES FROM THE BIBLE," "LITERARY ATTRACTIONS," ETC.

PHILADELPHIA:
PRESBYTERIAN BOARD OF PUBLICATION,
No. 821 CHESTNUT STREET.

STEREOTYPED BY WILLIAM W. HARDING, PHILADELPHIA.

PREFACE.

THE great saving truths of the gospel ought to be none the less attractive because they are old and familiar. They are indeed only the more precious because so many human hearts through all ages have believed them, and drawn consolation from them in life and in death. The story of the cross can never lose its interest or its power in a world of sin and death; and increasing millions every day bear witness to the truth of the prediction—"I, if I be lifted up, will draw all men unto myself."

The present volume is but one among the thousand attempts which have been made, and to the end of time, will continue to be made, to unfold the beauties of Immanuel, and to show forth that attractive power by which he draws a dying world to himself. No mortal pen is adequate to such a task. And yet it is permitted, even to the humblest, to approach, to behold, to admire, and then to tell, at least something of his glory. It is in the person and character of Immanuel, that we find the very essence of our faith. He is himself faith's great and all-satisfying object. We tell the story of salvation just as we tell of Jesus—the facts of his life, death, sufferings, instructions, resurrection, and ascension to glory. We hope for life and glory beyond the grave only in proportion as our faith can rest on him.

With such convictions the writer has approached this matchless theme, and has studied to unfold it, not in the lights of speculation and fancy, but only in that clear and sacred light which shines from the inspired pages. He would seek to commend to every dying fellow man, the personal character of the Redeemer, as infinitely the most lovely and attractive object that was ever revealed to the contemplation of the human mind. But while commending it thus as containing our only possible hope of salvation, he has sought to present it in no other way than as it has been revealed to us by those who "beheld his glory, the glory as of the Only-begotten of the Father, full of grace and truth."

CONTENTS.

CHAPTER X.

CHAPTER XI.

CHAPTER XII.

CHAPTER XIII.

THE BEAUTY OF IMMANUEL.

"HIS NAME SHALL BE CALLED WONDERFUL"

CHAPTER I.

THE LIFE AND CHARACTER OF JESUS CHRIST.

FROM all the characters portrayed in the Bible or exemplified in human history, it is a sublime ascent to that of Jesus Christ. In a former volume* it has been our aim to trace the streams of holy influence, so grand and beautiful, as they flowed forth over all the ancient world, in the lives of heroes and sages, kings and statesmen, prophets and apostles. We must now rise to the fountain head. We have been gazing on the stars of the greater and the lesser magnitudes, as for four thousand years they rose and set in the mighty firmament; we must now behold the bright beams of the Sun of Righteousness, as he rises to set no more, in the clear and perfect day of a finished apocalypse. All that was lovely and of good report in these diversified characters of four thousand years, was but a preparation of the mind

* "Life Pictures from the Bible."

of man for the unfolding of that one perfect character, to which they all in a manner pointed, and from which they had in fact by anticipation borrowed all their brightness. For it is not more certain that human hearts began to be inspired with elevating hopes by that first promise in Eden of a Saviour to come, than it is that human character began to be moulded to forms of greatness and beauty by the conception, dim and shadowy as it may have been at first, of God manifest in the flesh. So that we must regard the character of Immanuel, not only as sending down its influences over the eighteen centuries that have followed, but as throwing back its rays to the very gates of the primeval paradise, and giving a brighter glow to every saintly and heroic character that adorned the patriarchal and prophetic ages.

They all rejoiced to see his day, though afar off: and they were enabled to shine as lights in a dark world, because they were themselves illuminated by faith in a God incarnate—even that glorious living Redeemer of whom Job spoke, who should stand in the latter day upon the earth.

Regarded simply in a literary and historical point of view, the character of Jesus of Nazareth is the wonder and the study of all ages. Regarded only in that light, it would be the greatest enigma that ever appeared in the annals of man. Taking his life and actions as recorded in the New Testament. and looking upon him merely as we would any other historical personage, aside from any claim to a supernatural mission and a Divine nature; we have both a career and a character, to which there is nothing in the past history of our race that affords the slightest parallel, and for which nothing in any of the known elements of human nature offers the slightest solution. It is not only unique and original: it is infinitely the most unique and original thing that has ever been seen on earth. It is such an originality, as the forty centuries which went before, though constantly foretelling it, never produced; and the eighteen that have followed, have never found a duplicate. In the progress of nearly six thousand years, it has appeared but once; and with all man's improvement and vaunted approaches to perfection, there is not the slightest probability that it will ever appear again, until He shall appear according to his promise. It is not more certain, that there is one God only over universal nature, than it is, that there is but one Jesus Christ in all history. Simply as a man, he stands at an infinite distance from every other man of our race: even as the Bible says, "holy, harmless, undefiled, and separate from sinners."

It is said that the great masters of painting and statuary, in embodying their highest conception of perfection in the "human form divine," do not take the idea from any one living man, but from a thousand different subjects—combining the beauty and the strength and all the manly virtues of each, into one symmetrical and glorious form. But the character of Jesus Christ was not the result of any such combination as this. It is most true that it was gradually unfolded in all the prophecies, through a period of four thousand years, brighter and brighter glimpses of it being caught from age to age, and even impersonated in those great characters which typified his own; but then it was not unfolded by man working upon man, and adding the excellences of a Cicero to those of a Socrates, or even the higher virtues of a Moses to those of a Paul, but by God himself revealing a pattern of moral beauty from the skies, and thus giving the world assurance of a style of humanity, which had otherwise never been known to man. For certain it is, that the great masters of this world's wisdom, who through sixty centuries have been working upon man outside of the Bible, and independently as they think of its aid, have never, by any blending of the virtues of the great, or otherwise, produced even in fiction, such a character as the Christ of the old Testament prophets, and the Christ of the New Testament history.

But it is not merely in a literary and historical point of view, that we now propose to contemplate his wonderful character. It is in the full light of all the Scriptures, both of the Old Testament and the New, that we must estimate his character. We are not at liberty to ignore any part of the work and revelation of God. If we admit the Christ of history at all, we must admit the whole Christ of revelation. The moment we behold the veritable living man Christ Jesus, we are bound to recognize and adore all that belonged to him and marked him as something more than a man. His whole character—his whole august and mysterious nature, human and divine—stands before us as distinctly in the Bible, as any living personage was ever revealed to the eyes or the conceptions of men. It is Jesus Immanuel who is the burden of all the Scriptures. It is not one like Abraham, or Moses, or David, or Daniel, or John the Baptist: but one, the latchet of whose shoes they were not worthy to unloose: not a helpless sinner of our race like the greatest of these, but one who is the Saviour of every sinner of the race who will trust in him: one, dwelling indeed in human form, like unto his brethren the sons of men, but in whom dwelleth all the fulness of the Godhead bodily. If it is the child of Bethlehem, the son of Joseph, the man of Nazareth, the sufferer of Calvary, who is called Jesus; let us not forget that it is the Wonderful, the Counsellor, the mighty God, the everlasting Father, the Prince of peace, who is called Jesus. And we can no more set aside one class of the facts than we can the other. If we take the human and reject the Divine, or take the Divine and reject the human, we do it at our peril; for in either case we reject the testimony of God concerning his Son, and the only offer of God for our salvation.

Now it is remarkable, that the proofs of the humanity and the Divinity of Jesus Christ are not only alike full and explicit in the Scriptures, but they are everywhere mingled together in exact proportions, and stated in precisely similar terms. If there is any point which is made plain, and guarded against the ingenuity and sophisms of unbelief, it would seem to be this. How do we know that Jesus of Nazareth was a man? By his being called a man, and exercising all the functions, attributes, and works of man. He is called the man of sorrows, the son of man, the child born—born of the virgin Mary, suffered under Pontius Pilate, crucified, dead, and buried. He eats, drinks, walks, sleeps, feels, thinks, suffers, and dies as a man; and therefore he is a man. And how do we know he is God? Precisely in the same way. He is called God, wears all the titles of God—the Mighty God—does all the works of God—assumes all the attributes of God—receives from men and angels in earth and heaven, the very worship of God. He is conceived of the Holy Ghost, announced at his birth as the Saviour of the world, attested from heaven as the Son of God, condemned to death for making himself God; raised from the dead, justified by the Spirit, seen of angels, preached unto the Gentiles, believed on in the world, received up into glory as God manifest in the flesh. He speaks, acts, lives, reigns, and triumphs over all as God; and therefore he is God.

Following the method hitherto pursued in all our illustrations of Bible characters, which is to let them speak and act for themselves as near as we can in the very terms of the sacred oracles, let us now address ourselves to this last and highest task —which is to set forth a brief but comprehensive outline of the life and the adorable character of Immanuel. And may the Spirit of all truth fill our hearts and minds with some measure of that conception of it which inspired the undertaking of the beloved disciple when he said, "The word was made flesh and dwelt among us, and we beheld his glory, the glory as of the only begotten of the Father, full of grace and truth."

CHAPTER II.

HIS BIRTH AND EARLY HISTORY.

We need not stop to recite here the wonderful story of Bethlehem, which is so familiar to every child. Perhaps nothing in all the Bible is so universally known. The shepherds watching their flocks by night, the angel from heaven declaring his birth that day, the multitude of the heavenly host praising God in the highest, the star pointing out his birth-place, the wise men from the East seeking to find him, the babe lying in the manger at Bethlehem, the gold, frankincense, and myrrh offered to him, the cruel edict of King Herod, the warnings from God to the wise men and to Joseph, the presentation of the child to the Lord in the temple at Jerusalem, the timely flight into Egypt, and the safe return to Nazareth—all this we have heard from our lisping infancy. But though it has been told ten thousand thousand times, it shall never lose its graphic power and beauty as a narrative, nor its interest as the opening chapter in the scheme of God's salvation. It stands just where it ought to stand on the introductory pages of the New Testament. It is the pure and crystal fountain, sparkling with the waters of immortal life for man, out of which the life of the Son of God on earth is to flow, and to which all nations shall come to drink. Since the creation of Adam no human life had ever had so wonderful a beginning. And now at the distance of eighteen centuries and a half, there is to us as deep an interest in it, as to those who first received the glad tidings, "Unto you is born this day in the city of David, a Saviour who is Christ the Lord," and heard the song of an innumerable host above, "Glory to God in the highest, peace on earth, and good will to men."

It was the fulfilment of those deep prophecies of Isaiah, which for eight centuries hitherto had found no adequate solution. "Behold a virgin shall conceive and bear a son, and shall call his name Immanuel. For unto us a child is born, unto us a son is given; and the government shall be upon his shoulder." It was the beginning of the fulfilment of that still more ancient oracle which had come down from the garden of Eden. "The seed of the woman shall bruise the serpent's head." Loud and fierce has been the outcry which modern infidelity has raised against this simple and unvarnished narrative of our Lord's conception and nativity, in the opening pages of the New Testament. But we submit that such a conception and nativity as this is precisely the thing which the ancient prophecies called for, and without which those prophecies, not only never have been, but never can be fulfilled.

And we submit again, that on the supposition that those prophecies had a meaning in them and were ever to be fulfilled at all, by one who was Immanuel, God with us, God incarnate, God manifest in the flesh, the account of our Saviour's birth in the New Testament, as one made of a woman, "conceived by the Holy Ghost, and born of the virgin Mary," is not only a true and exact fulfilment, but one which commends itself to our reason as eminently befitting all the conditions and possibilities of the case. It is precisely what we should expect to occur, and precisely the manner in which we should say it ought to occur, if the prophecies of four thousand years are ever to be verified in fact, and the Deity is ever to be arrayed in mortal flesh. Given the fact of an incarnation of the Divine nature, and then the fact, that the incarnate one is to be a virgin-born child, and a real man with a true body and a reasonable soul like ourselves; and what other plan will our worldly wise philosophy devise for its accomplishment more worthy of God's infinite wisdom and man's belief, than the one recorded by Matthew and Luke? "This is the Lord's doing and it is marvellous in our eyes." But so far from discrediting the New Testament as given of God, it is a confirmation of it; because it corresponds to every conception of the Messiah as revealed in the Old Testament; and its very unlikeness to anything that man could have done, or would have invented, is a voucher of its truth. A

Divine religion, conscious of the truth of God, could unfearingly go forth with that high and marvellous mystery on its very forehead. A false religion, as our sensitive and shame-faced unbelief shows, would have shrunk with scorn from inventing such a story, supposing it to be a fiction, and still more from the shame of telling it, supposing it to be a fact. That the Evangelists have told it, not only without fear or shrinking, but with exultation and joy, and that, upon the very face of their sacred books, and in the eyes of a proud and incredulous world, is itself a demonstration that it is not of men, but of God.

It was in the reign of Cæsar Augustus, the Roman emperor, that this great event took place. It was a time of peace over all the world—fit time for the advent of him who was the Prince of Peace. The temple of Janus at Rome, after the ceaseless conflict of ages, was now closed, as indicative that the world was at peace: and the temple at Jerusalem, spared by the haughty invader, was still open for that morning and evening sacrifice, which had so long foreshadowed the Lamb of God, that should take away the sin of the world. The very fulness of time had come—the prophecies all ripe for fulfilment, the Jewish nation looking for its deliverer, the world at large full of expectation, and the preparation of four thousand years now completed Thus at the precise point of time, and at the proper place, at Bethlehem of Judah, and of David's royal line, glorious still though in obscurity, and of a virgin mother overshadowed by the Holy Ghost, and under outward circumstances of deepest humiliation combined with others of unearthly grandeur, was Jesus the Messiah born. It is no marvel to us that a child thus born should be a wonder and a study to all who saw him and heard of him—that his kinswoman Elizabeth and his virgin mother and the no longer incredulous Zacharias, should be filled with the Holy Ghost and utter songs of joy at his birth, that the shepherds should go home glorifying and praising God for all the things that they had heard and seen, that sages from the farthest east should come to worship and adore him, that the guilty Herod should be conscious that the rightful claimant of his throne was born, that the aged Simeon and Anna waiting at the temple for the consolation of Israel, as soon as they beheld him, should rejoice, and say, "Lord, now lettest thou thy servant depart in peace according to thy word, for mine eyes have seen thy salvation," and that Joseph and his mother should deeply ponder all these things in their hearts. Had Abraham who rejoiced to see his day, and the dying Jacob who told of his descent from Judah, and Isaiah who spake of his glory, and Micah who marked his birth-place, and Daniel who designated the time, been there, they too, like Simeon and Anna, would have felt that it was enough—this is the Son of the Highest, the

Prince of the house of David, the glory of Israel, and a light to lighten the Gentiles.

From these scenes of his early infancy, until he was twelve years old, the sacred record is almost entirely silent. After his presentation in the temple, the flight into Egypt, and the return to Nazareth on the death of Herod, our only information is that "the child grew and waxed strong in spirit, filled with wisdom, and the grace of God was upon him." But this is enough to show he was preparing for his great life work. We know that his parents neglected nothing within their power, for we are told that they did all things according to the law, and were accustomed to go up every year to Jerusalem to attend the passover. After all that had been communicated both by the angel and the prophets of the Lord, and after all that she had herself spoken by the Holy Ghost, his mother would not fail to use every means of instruction in the sacred oracles, and to inculcate every lesson of early piety, that this child should be trained for his sublime mission as the Son of the Highest.

Accordingly the Evangelist Luke gives us one striking and beautiful incident, occurring at the age of twelve, to illustrate how during all this early period he had, indeed, waxed strong in spirit, filled with celestial wisdom and grace divine.

His parents, whom he had accompanied to Jerusalem were returning from the great annual feast in the caravan of their kinsfolk and acquaintance.

Unknown to them Jesus had tarried behind. Missing him, but supposing that he was safe in the company, (for, doubtless, all knew him and felt an interest in so extraordinary a child,) they went a day's journey, and then turned back in search of him. It was not until after three days that they found him. He was in the temple, sitting in the midst of the doctors, both hearing them and asking them questions. And all that heard him were astonished at his understanding and answers. Mary and Joseph were amazed: and she said, "Son, why hast thou thus dealt with us? Behold, thy father and I have sought thee sorrowing." And he said, "How is it that ye sought me? Wist ye not that I must be about my Father's business?" They did not fully comprehend his answer; but, as if to show that it was in no spirit of disobedience to them, his earthly parents, that he had acted thus, it is added, "He went down with them, and came to Nazareth, and was subject unto them. But his mother kept all these sayings in her heart. And Jesus increased in wisdom and stature, and in favour with God and man."

CHAPTER III.

HIS BAPTISM AND PUBLIC MINISTRY.

When our Saviour had reached the age of thirty, the time of life at which the Jewish priests were accustomed to enter upon their public functions, conscious that it became him to fulfil all righteousness under that dispensation in which he was born, and that the hour was at hand for him to be made manifest to Israel as the Messiah, and to enter publicly upon the discharge of all the offices of that great work for which he had come into the world, he left Nazareth and came to John, the son of Zacharias, in the wilderness of Judea, to be baptized of him. John, surrounded by the ten thousands of Israel, was on the banks of the Jordan, whither he had gone to preach the baptism of repentance, and to fulfil his own high mission, as the voice of one crying in the wilderness, and the messenger who should prepare the way of the Lord before him. Knowing that this was the immaculate Son of the Highest, and that, as such, he could have no need of that baptism of repentance which he was sent to preach, John, at first refused to administer the ordinance to him. But being admonished that it was necessary in order to fulfil all the requirements of the law, he suffered it to be so, and thus publicly in the eyes of Israel, and in virtue of his own prophetic and priestly office, administered that solemn rite which marks the era of the Messiah's introduction into his public ministry, and to which he himself was accustomed to appeal as the very seal of authority, when the Jews disputed his legal rights in the temple.

As a public inauguration of his ministry, nothing could be more appropriate and imposing than this baptism. A king in virtue of his being of David's royal line, a prophet and a priest in virtue of his being anointed by the Holy Ghost, and now publicly designated by John, he had both the testimony of earth and heaven, that he was the Messiah. John saw and bare record that this is the Son of God; crying to the thousands of Israel, "Behold the Lamb of God that taketh away the sin of the world." And he had a far higher testimony than John's, even that of the Father and the Holy Ghost. That august attestation is recorded in the following words: "Now when all the people were baptized (a people thus prepared for the Lord), it came to pass, that Jesus also being baptized and praying, the heaven was opened unto him. And the Holy Ghost descended in a bodily shape, like a dove, upon him, and a voice came from heaven which said, Thou art my beloved Son; in thee I am well pleased."

Thus attested and honoured by God and man, thus endowed plentifully with all Divine and human gifts, thus consecrated and anointed to the sublimest mission ever known to man, thus publicly proclaimed to Israel by his great forerunner, and thus, while the dew of youth was fresh upon him, and all the strength of opening manhood bounded in his veins, did Jesus Immanuel begin his work.

His first great work was one of conflict. Its arena was in the unseen and spiritual world. He had come to destroy the works of the Devil; to repair the evils which he had wrought, to atone for the guilt which man through him had incurred. He had undertaken for man—he had come to be God's Advocate and man's Redeemer. And so the battle began with the powers of the darkness of this world—a struggle for the mastery between the incarnate Son of God, and him who, from the beginning, had been God's adversary and man's enemy. Crowned with all the glories of his recent baptism, strong in the confidence of God's favour, and full of the Holy Ghost, our blessed Lord is led away by the spirit that was upon him, not to the abodes of men, but to the deep solitudes of the wilderness, there to meet the enemy of our souls, there to be tempted of the devil. And there, single-handed and alone, amid fastings and hungerings which no mortal flesh but his could have endured, for forty days he wrestles with the prince of the power of the air, the god of this world. We shall not stay to depict the various changes of the solemn scene, as it is detailed by the evangelists. Brief as the sacred record is, and short as was its period of forty days, it has furnished the ground work of Milton's second great epic, Paradise Regained. And when that conflict was ended, and from every assault of the tempter, the Son of God had come off a conqueror, the gifted bard represents the great battle as fought, the victory won, the tempter foiled, lost Paradise restored, and "Eden raised in the waste wilderness." But this is certainly a great misconception of the work of Christ. The work was not finished, nor the great conflict ended with the forty days in the wilderness. It was but just begun, to be renewed and perpetuated through his whole earthly career. And so with deep significance, one of the Evangelists tells us, that "when the devil had ended all the temptations, he departed from him for a season." And then angels came and ministered unto him.

But this first great conflict being past, the next scene of his labours was among men. He had a work of love to do among men, as well as a war to wage with the devil. Hence we follow him from the wilderness as he returns in the power of the Spirit into Galilee; preaching the gospel of the kingdom and healing all manner of diseases among the people. Through all the cities, and in all the synagogues of Galilee, the great burden of his message is, "The time is fulfilled, the kingdom of heaven is at hand; repent ye and believe the gospel." When entreated by the people in one place not to depart from them, he replies, "I must preach the kingdom of God to other cities also; for therefore am I sent." And with such words of power and wisdom, grace and truth, did he preach, that the people were everywhere astonished at his doctrine, and followed him from city to city and even into the deserts to attend upon his extraordinary ministry. Among the important opening acts of this public ministry, he called and ordained his twelve disciples, that they might be with him to receive his instructions in all the mysteries of the kingdom of heaven, and that he might send them forth likewise to preach the gospel to the lost sheep of the house of Israel. It was also at an early stage of this ministry, that he went back to Nazareth where he had been brought up, and on the Sabbath day read in their synagogue that remarkable passage from Isaiah which was then accomplished in himself, "The Spirit of the Lord is upon me, because he hath anointed me to preach the gospel to the poor; he hath sent me to heal the broken hearted, to preach deliverance to the captives, and recovering of sight to the blind, to set at liberty them that are bruised, to preach the acceptable year of the Lord." And, as he said unto them, "This day is this Scripture fulfilled in your ears, they all bare him witness, and wondered at the gracious words which proceeded out of his mouth."

And yet, before he was done, with such pungent power and zeal for God did he preach the truth to these self-righteous sinners of Nazareth, that, as if prophetical of the manner in which an unbelieving world would in all ages treat the messages and ministers of God, they were filled with wrath, and thrust him out of their city.

It is no part of our plan to follow him step by step through his whole public ministry. This would require volumes. It was a ministry of incessant labours, extending through more than three years, from his baptism to the hour, when, hanging on the cross, he said, "It is finished." It was brief, as compared with that of the great body of his ministers in all ages of the church. But whether we consider its sublime beginning or its still sublimer close, whether we consider the mighty manifestations of Divine power which attended it from first to last, or the mighty results and influences which have flowed from it through all subsequent ages, it stands alone, unapproached and unapproachable in its solitary grandeur. No public teacher, no preacher of righteousness, by any ministry long or short, ever made such an impression on the mind of man. By an unfailing attendance upon all the great annual feasts at Jerusalem, by incessant journeys through Galilee, Samaria, Judea, and the region beyond the Jordan, by public and private discourses in season and out of season wherever he went, the strong probability is that, during these three years, the vast body of his countrymen, as well as thousands from other nations, had listened to his matchless instructions. "The people which sat in darkness saw a great light, and to those who sat in the region and shadow of death, light was sprung up."

We have one of his great public discourses recorded at length—the sermon on the Mount—delivered to his disciples and the countless multitudes that had come from all the cities of Galilee, Judea, and the region beyond Jordan—delivered not in any building, for there was none in the land large enough to hold the people, but in the open air, on the broad terraces of a mountain. And this is perhaps given as an example of the matter, style, manner, and surroundings of his ordinary popular discourses. Whether, therefore, we consider the deep and thrilling interest of the doctrines which he taught, or the words of grace and power with which he spoke, or the mighty works with which he called attention to his preaching, or the fact that both in Galilee and at all the great festivals of Jerusalem, he was always attended by an immense multitude, numbering sometimes, even in remote desert places, four and five thousand men, we must conclude that there were few, if any, of his cotemporaries from Dan to Beersheba, who had not heard, or had the opportunity of hearing this great teacher.

Now, in this wonderful ministry, taken as a whole, we notice three great attributes, everywhere prominent, which at once illustrate the character of our blessed Master, and present him as a perfect model for all who would preach the Gospel.

The first is his consuming and self-sacrificing zeal for God. "My meat is to do the will of him that sent me, and to finish his work." "I must work the works of him that sent me while it is day; the night cometh when no man can work." From the day in which the Spirit of the Lord was poured upon him in double measure, anointing him to preach the Gospel to the poor, to his expiring breath on the cross, his life was one great act of consecration to God in the work he had given him to do. In this spirit his days were spent in incessant toil, and at night when others slept, he retired to the mountains or the deserts to pray. When countless thousands were following him from city to city all over Galilee, and depriving him, not only of rest, but of opportunities for necessary food, Mark tells us, that his friends went out to lay hold upon him, thinking that he was beside him. But what were friends and kindred to him, who could say, "Let the dead bury their dead, but come thou and follow me?" "I have a baptism to be baptized with, and how am I straitened till it be accomplished!" "The Son of man came not to be ministered unto, but to minister, and to give his life a ransom for many." "Whosoever shall do the will of God, the same is my brother and sister and mother." In this spirit he could appropriate the prophecy as true of his whole ministry: "The zeal of thy house hath eaten me up." And thus he said at the last, "Father, I have glorified thee on the earth, I have finished the work which thou gavest me to do."

The second great characteristic displayed through all his ministry was his intense and yearning love for his fellow-men. He beheld the multitudes and had compassion on them, for they were as sheep without a shepherd. But he was himself the good Shepherd. He was sent to the lost sheep of the house of Israel. He came to seek and to save that which was lost. His great life-work, as it regarded man, was to go about doing good—to labour for others, to suffer for others, to bear our griefs, and to carry our sorrows. In all our afflictions he was afflicted. The foxes had holes, and the birds of the air had nests, but the Son of man had not where to lay his head. His only home was with the friendless, his bed at night with the sons of the poor, his daily work to save the perishing. Thus he who was Lord of all, rich in all the treasures of the universe, and thought it no robbery to be equal with God, emptied himself of his glory, became poor for our sakes, condescended to men of low estate, and with a depth of compassion that had hitherto been unknown to men or angels, carried the offers of immortal life and glory in his own person to the wretched abodes of publicans and sinners. There is no trait of his character, no theme in all the Scriptures, on which his inspired apostles love more

3 *

to dwell, than this fulness of all Divine and human love in the bosom of Jesus. "The love of Christ constraineth us." It was in his life, as he healed the sick, raised the dead, cast out devils, preached the gospel to the poor, and answered the prayer of the dying sinner, even on the cross, that they beheld the highest manifestation of the Divine character, and learned the lesson—God is love.

While holding daily communion with God, such as the world knew not of, he was, at the same time, in intense sympathy with suffering man; his soul was all alive to human want and woe in every shape and form. He was touched with the feeling of our infirmities. He looked upon us in our lost estate with all the yearning tenderness of a brother's heart. He never sent the poor sorrowing suppliant empty away. Through his whole public ministry he was never too engaged to turn away from the cry for mercy. Through life, and in death itself, he had a heart to feel for sinners, and a hand that was ready to bring salvation. Even on the cross he could speak words of comfort to his heart-broken mother, open the gates of paradise to the dying thief, and for his murderers pray, "Father, forgive them, for they know not what they do." At the grave of Lazarus he wept with the weeping sisters, and over Jerusalem—loved and lost Jerusalem—chosen city of his God and Father—city of David and all the prophets, which, even for their sakes, he would have died to save—over Jerusalem, when her day was passed, he stood and cried in all the bitterness of yearning love—"O Jerusalem! Jerusalem! Thou that killest the prophets, and stonest them which are sent unto thee, how often would I have gathered thy children together, as a hen doth gather her chickens under her wings, but ye would not!" What a spectacle of love and pity was that!

"The Son of God in tears
  Angels with wonder see.
Be thou astonished, O my soul,
  He shed those tears for thee!
He wept that we might weep,
  Each sin demands a tear;
In heaven alone no sin is found,
  And there's no weeping there."

The third signal characteristic of his ministry, was the calm, unfearing, and unfaltering purpose, with which, from the opening to the close, he pursued his great work of devotion to God and good will to men. His life, in all its plans, purposes, and results, was a perfect, symmetrical, and consistent whole. He did all that he came to do—suffered all that he came to suffer. Though he saw the end from the beginning, and knew the cup of suffering which he must drink, he yet went steadily on without vacillation or shadow of turning. It is wonderful to notice how many opportunities to change his purpose pressed upon his pathway, and how many agencies, both of friends and foes, combined their power to divert him from his course. The temptations of the devil, the opposition of the wicked, the worldly expectations of his countrymen, the carnal hopes of his disciples, the readiness of the people to crown him as their king, the legions of angels that would have come at his call—these and a thousand other things conspired to any other result rather than that which occurred—a life of poverty and toil, and a death of agony. But through them all, and in despite of them all, he pressed his solitary way to the death of the cross. And, though he had often predicted it to his disciples, yet there was not a living being in the world who seemed capable of understanding the grand purpose that filled his own soul. There is something august and imposing in this position of solitary grandeur in which he stood even while thronged by living men. The evangelists are careful to tell us more than once, that his disciples understood not his sayings at the time. And then again behold him in his onward and unfaltering course. Though surrounded by enemies, and by dangers, thickening and growing more formidable at every step, he calmly faces them all, and walks unmoved amid the assaults of earth and hell, as one who feels immortal till his work be done. When warned by the Pharisees to flee from Galilee, because the blood-stained Herod would seek to kill him, his reply was, "Go ye and tell that fox, Behold I cast out devils and I do cures to-day and to-morrow; and the third day I shall be perfected. Nevertheless, I must walk to-day and to-morrow and the day (that is year) following; for it cannot be that a prophet perish out of Jerusalem." When at last, assaulted by all his foes and deserted by all his followers, he stood calm, silent, and alone before the judgment-seat of imperial Rome, and when the haughty Pilate, insolent with power, thought to overawe and intimidate him with the words—"Speakest thou not unto me? Knowest thou not that I have power to crucify thee, and have power to release thee?" his only answer was an inculcation of the doctrine of God's providence and man's impotence, "Thou couldst have no power at all against me, except it were given thee from above; therefore he that delivered me unto thee hath the greater sin."

These three great attributes, supreme love to God, good will to man, and heroic courage in the path of duty, so seldom combined in the character of men, and yet so essential to the development of the highest virtue, shone forth in the person of Immanuel in all their fulness and glory. On a lower scale, and so far as that which is human may imitate the Divine, the very same attributes adorned the character of the Apostle Paul, and by their combination made him the greatest of all the apostles. And so in all ages of the church, those who have been called to be partakers in the labours and trials of that ministry which he so gloriously illustrated, have excelled in power and abounded in usefulness, just in proportion as they have trodden in the footsteps and imitated all the imitable perfections of the Great Master.

CHAPTER IV.

HIS MIGHTY MIRACLES.

One of the most striking things attending the ministry of our blessed Lord, from its opening to its close, was the constant display of Divine power, by which even to the eyes of a gainsaying and unbelieving world he vindicated his claims as the Son of God and the Messiah of Israel. These displays were so numerous and so stupendous, that it seems never to have occurred to any one of his cotemporaries, whether Roman, Greek, or Jew, however incredulous or inimical, to evade their force by denying their reality. That was a device reserved for the ingenious sophistry of a later age. All that the eye and ear witnesses of his own times ever attempted to do, was to set aside the conclusions drawn from them touching his Divine mission, by ascribing them to some other agency than that of God. But in our day, such are the tactics of unbelief, that it is easier to deny their historical verity altogether, than to trust them into the hands of an inexorable logic, whose demands are infinitely better satisfied with the solution of the agency of God than with any other solution whatsoever.

King Herod, when he heard of these things, accounted for them by saying, "It is John the Baptist, who is risen from the dead; therefore mighty works do show forth themselves in him." The Pharisees who beheld them, said: "This man casteth out devils by Beelzebub the prince of the devils." The Roman centurion, who had gone through all the wonders of the cross and the sepulchre, could draw no other conclusion, than that this was "truly the Son of God." Nicodemus, a master in Israel, had arrived at the same conclusion long before: "No man can do these miracles that thou doest except God be with him." But modern rationalism, too proud to follow the superstitious credulity either of Herod or the Pharisees, and too undevout to confess with Nicodemus and the centurion, that this is the finger of God, seeks relief from argument and an easy solution of all the facts, by denying that the facts ever existed. The solution is short enough, and it might ere long, perhaps, find admirers, were it not that the facts have been reported on evidence which can never be set aside without overthrowing the truth of all history.

It is not our province here to enter upon the discussion of this evidence. Nor is it needful. It is enough to say, that the facts of the gospel history, both its ordinary and its extraordinary facts, are established on the testimony of witnesses as numerous and as competent as any in the annals of human history. The gospel history is a record of innumerable facts, great and small, occurring in the ordinary course of human affairs, which no mortal ever thought of questioning, though we know them on the authority of that record alone. It is, at the same time, a record of many extraordinary or supernatural facts, including all the mighty miracles of our Saviour's life, which no mortal would have ever thought of questioning any more than the others, except for their being out of the ordinary course of human events. But it is to be observed, that our knowledge and belief of the two classes of facts rest precisely on the same ground—which, indeed, is the ground of all history—the testimony of competent witnesses. For the mighty miracles of Christ and all the supernatural events of the New Testament, we have as many infallible proofs and as many competent witnesses, as we have for all its ordinary events, great and small; because the witnesses and the proofs are precisely the same for both. The historians who tell us Jesus lived and died, are the same who tell us that he rose from the dead and ascended to heaven. On what ground then are they to be believed in the one case and discredited in the other? Nay, more, the world is compelled to credit their testimony on all these ordinary historical facts, because there are other witnesses outside of the Bible who avouch the same, and the keenest criticism of eighteen centuries has never yet convicted them of falsehood on any known historical event. On what ground then does infidelity set aside their testimony, on certain great facts lying outside of the domain of secular history, when on a thousand things lying within the domain of that history, infidelity is compelled to admit that they have always reported the truth, and never once spoken falsely? For the man who credits the general voice of history, and credits even the historians of the new Testament on a thousand minor points, and then deliberately rejects all the great points on which they give their most solemn and emphatic testimony, the only fitting answer is that of the Master himself on another occasion: "Out of thine own mouth will I condemn thee, thou wicked servant."

But, as touching the credibility of the miracles of Christ, it should certainly go far to vindicate their claims, even at the bar of the most sceptical philosophy, to consider the person by whom and the object for which they were wrought. All the parts of the gospel history have an intrinsic fitness and harmony with each other; and its facts are no more to be judged of singly and disjunctively, than are the facts of Astronomy or any other science to be judged of out of their connections and harmonious adaptations. Now let this principle be applied to the miracles of Christ. And who will deny—supposing it to be possible for God to display his mighty power on earth, and probable that he would ever do it—that the incarnation of the Son of God was an occasion worthy of the exercise of that miraculous power. By whom ought signs and wonders and mighty works to be done, if not by God manifest in the flesh? And for what ends ought they to be wrought, if not that he, with all the overflowing bounty of a God, might pour salvation upon the perishing, and vindicate to men and angels his amazing mission of love and mercy in this guilty world? Once admit the fact of the presence of the incarnate Son of God on earth, and you have an occasion, an object, and an agent, worthy of all these displays of Divine power. Once conceive of Jesus of Nazareth as being all that he claimed to be, and all the prophets said, and so far from its being an incredible thing that he should raise the dead or do anything else which God can do, the more he displays these mighty powers, the more easily can we believe in him. In this state of things —in the presence of Immanuel—God with us—we ascend at once into a higher and purer realm of being, where miracle is the recognized law, and the ordinary course of things would be anomalous and abnormal. When God works, it is easier for man to believe with miracles than without them.

Familiarized to displays of Divine power, as the Jewish mind had been by the whole past history of the nation, it was still filled with astonishment and awe at the miracles of Christ. The amazement arose not from the fact that such works should be done; for, on that score, a Jew had nothing to doubt; but that one who belonged to the common people, a man without profession or learning, an humble Galilean, whom many had known from his childhood, should do such works. Wherever he went the people marvelled, saying, "It was never so seen in Israel." When he came into his own country, they were still more astonished, saying, "Whence hath this man this wisdom and these mighty works? Is not this the carpenter's son? Is not his mother called Mary? and his brethren James, and Joses, and Simon, and Judas? And his sisters, are they not all with us? Whence then hath this man all these things?" Though this was the language of unbelief, it still shows how deep was the feeling of wonder in the public mind touching these mighty works. The wonder was natural enough, at least at the first. For, on the one hand, here was everything in the outward condition, history, and circumstances of the young Nazarene forbidding the thought that he could be the great Prophet of Israel whose coming had been foretold from the first; and, on the other, here were all, and more than all, the mighty works that any prophet had ever wrought by the power of God.

The most usual designation of these miracles in the gospel history is that of signs, wonders, and mighty works. The fundamental idea of the Greek word, translated miracle, is that of *power*, *strength*, *force*. Where, for example, Christ is called the "power of God," it is the same word which in the New Testament is so often rendered miracle. These mighty works of Christ, therefore, while they are called *wonders*, as referring to their effects upon the minds of men, and *signs*, as referring to the object for which they were wrought, are, strictly and properly, as referring to their inherent nature and origin, *powers*, because they display the direct, immediate, and almighty power of God.

Nothing is clearer from the sacred narrative, than the great moral purpose with which all the miracles of Christ were performed. They all, from the first of them, the turning of water into wine in Cana of Galilee, down to the last of them, the restoration of the ear of Malchus by a touch on the night of his betrayal, had a distinct public character, and the same great end in view. As such, they all belonged to his public ministry, and formed an essential part of it. They were not wrought, any of them, for his own personal convenience, or the accommodation of his disciples. But from the first to the last, they were all intended, even including those in which he fed the hungry multitudes, relieved the maladies of the sick, and raised the dead, to manifest to Israel the presence and glory of their Messiah—to convince his disciples and the world, that he was himself the anointed Christ of God even in this state of deepest humiliation. And as to the number and the glory of these displays of Divine power, during his three years' ministry, it is manifest, that just enough were given to answer the purpose and no more. On the one hand he was not sparing of his miracles, when they were needed; on the other, he was not prodigal of them where they were not. At some places they were so abundant, that the sick were conveyed to him from the housetops, and there went forth healing virtue from the very hem of his garment. At others, we are told, that he could do no mighty work there because of their unbelief. It is easy to see, that one who possessed the power which Jesus did, could have wielded that power indefinitely. He who could raise the dead, in three different instances, at intervals probably of a year—first of a maiden just dead—then of a young man borne on his bier to the tomb—and then of one dead four days and buried, could have opened every grave in Palestine and filled the world with proofs of his Godhead. But how then should the Scriptures have been fulfilled, and the work of man's redemption accomplished? It is easy to see, that while his miracles could not well have been less numerous and glorious than they were, in consistency with the vindication of his character and mission as the Son of God; at the same time they could not well have been more so, in consistency with that estate of humiliation and suffering, for which he came into the world. And thus on certain occasions of the brighter manifestations of his Divinity, we find him charging his disciples not to make them known till he should be risen from the dead. More miracles and brighter visions of his glory, would have overshadowed his humanity altogether, and defeated the great end of his incarnation and humiliation. But the great end for which all his miracles were wrought was to convince men, as by the manifest testimony of God himself, that this was his Son, the Saviour of the world, though for a season veiled in mortal flesh. Thus John says of his opening miracle—"This beginning of miracles did Jesus in Cana of Galilee, and manifested forth his glory; and his disciples believed on him."

"This beginning of miracles," says Trench, "is as truly an introduction to all other miracles which Christ did, as the parable of the Sower is an introduction to all other parables which he spoke. No other miracle would have had so much in it of prophecy, would have served as so fit an inauguration to the whole future work of the Son of God. For that work might be characterized throughout as an ennobling of the common, and a transmuting of the mean—a turning of the water of earth into the wine of heaven." It is a little remarkable that the whole number of reported and minutely recorded miracles in the life of Jesus should so nearly correspond with the number of his parables. The parables, as enumerated by Trench, are thirty; while the miracles, including the one at the sea of Tiberias after his resurrection, are thirty-three. These are, in both cases, such only as the Evangelists have singled out from a countless multitude and recorded at length, as examples of all the rest. For they tell us that Jesus healed all manner of sicknesses and diseases among the people, and did many other signs in the presence of his disciples, which are not recorded by them, and could not be without filling the world with books.

This abundant manifestation of miraculous powers was looked upon by the people, as one of the infallible proofs of Messiahship. On a certain occasion, when the question was raised, whether Jesus were the Christ, we find some asking, as if to put the matter beyond all doubt, "When Christ cometh, will he do more miracles than those which this man hath done?" This is an incidental indication of the multitude of his mighty works. But there are many similar indications. For example, Luke mentions the case of a poor sick woman, who was healed by merely touching the border of his garment; and Mark gives us the following record —"And whithersoever he entered into any villages or cities or country, they laid the sick in the streets, and besought him that they might touch, if it were but the border of his garment; and as many as touched him were made whole." What an amazing manifestation of his fulness of Divine power was this, that the sick who thronged his pathway had but to touch his clothing in faith, in order to receive that healing virtue which went out of him! Who can imagine any higher credentials of the presence of the incarnate Deity than such trophies of his healing power? And once admit that he exercised such power, and who does not see how natural are all the recorded facts of the myriads upon myriads who left every thing to follow him, not only from city to city, but across the sea and into the barren deserts?

His prominent, and so to speak, representative miracles, are the following: The water made wine, the healing of the nobleman's son, the first miraculous draught of fishes, the stilling of the tempest, the demoniacs in the country of the Gadarenes, the raising of Jairus' daughter, the woman with an issue of blood, the opening of the eyes of two blind in the house, the healing of the paralytic, the cleansing of the leper, the healing of the centurion's servant, the demoniac in the synagogue of Capernaum, the healing of Simon's wife's mother, the raising of the widow's son, the healing of the impotent man at Bethesda, the miraculous feeding of five thousand, the walking on the sea, the opening of the eyes of one born blind, the restoring of a man with a withered hand, the woman with the spirit of infirmity, the healing of a man with a dropsy, the cleansing of the ten lepers, the healing of the daughter of the Syrophenician woman, the healing of one deaf and dumb, the miraculous feeding of four thousand, the opening of the eyes of one blind at Bethsaida, the healing of the lunatic child, the money in the fish's mouth, the raising of Lazarus, the opening of the eyes of two blind men near Jericho, the withering of the fruitless fig tree, the healing of Malchus's ear, and the second miraculous draught of fishes.

In this long list it is striking to notice, first, the vast variety of subjects on which our Lord exerted his almighty power. They were such as to show his absolute mastery over the whole realm of nature, animate and inanimate, physical and spiritual. Not only the elements of matter, but the spirits of living men and the powers of the invisible world were subject to his control. Not only the winds and the waves obeyed him, but the very laws of matter were reversed, or new properties created at his command; the water became wine, the sea solid beneath his feet, the loaves and fishes multiplied into food for thousands, the living fig tree died at his word, and a fish from the deep brought him tribute money. And not only diseases of the body, and defects of its organs existing from birth, but the deeper maladies of the mind and spirit, all departed at his bidding. And further still, as if this were not enough to show the range of his power, the demons of darkness fled from their long fettered victims at his approach, and in three well-attested instances the disembodied spirit came back to its tabernacle of clay, and the tomb gave up its dead. If the problem were whether this is the Son of God, and the trial had to be made again in the face of all the universe, and we were called upon to fix upon thirty or more different cases or occasions, which should be the tests of Almighty power, and proofs of a present Deity, we cannot imagine any thirty cases more to the point, and more utterly beyond the power of all the men in the universe to do, than precisely those things which Jesus did. For the very least of them involved a power as impossible to man as the creation of a world.

But there is a second feature pervading these mighty works, as remarkable as their infinite range of power. It is their character of benevolence and mercy. In this they differ greatly from many of the miracles of the ancient dispensation. The miracles of Moses, of Joshua, of Samuel, of Elijah, and all the prophets, while vindicating the truth of God, were oftentimes visitations of awful judgment and destruction. Not so the mighty works of Christ. They are a mirror to reflect all the milder glories of Immanuel's character as well as to assert his Divinity. If we had nothing but his miracles to judge from, we should have enough to show that God is love, and that his mission was one of infinite grace and mercy to our ruined race. For besides their higher purpose, which was to glorify God by vindicating the Divine mission of his well-beloved Son, they all, with a few exceptions, such as the tribute money and the barren fig tree, were selected with another end in view, which was to display the deep compassion of Immanuel's love, as the Friend of the friendless and the Saviour of sinners. Hence, if we look over this list, we shall find that they are mostly miracles of charity and mercy, wrought for the healing and the consolation of the poor, the sick, the outcast, the perishing—the wretched sons and daughters of affliction, for whom this world could do, and cared to do, nothing. More than two thirds of them are cases of healing and restoration—and that too of a character so aggravated as to lie utterly beyond the power of human aid. Eight of them are cases in which the Son of God exerted his mighty power, either at the solicitation or for the relief of some poor, suffering, and sorrowing woman. One of them was the humble Syrophenician woman who could not claim even to belong to the lost sheep of the house of Israel, and yet did not depart without his blessing.

Now, if we bear in mind that these recorded cases of the New Testament are given but as examples of all the other unnumbered signs, wonders, and mighty works which Jesus exhibited during his whole public ministry, we shall be constrained to confess, that they furnish a demonstration both of his Divine power and his superhuman excellence of character, which is absolutely perfect. And so he was accustomed to appeal to them, when the Jews demanded proof of his being the Christ, "The works that I do in my Father's name, they bear witness of me."

CHAPTER V.

HIS MATCHLESS INSTRUCTIONS.

It would be difficult to say which is the more remarkable of the two, and which contains a fuller revelation of the character of Immanuel—his mighty works or the words of grace and truth which he spake. The conclusion of Nicodemus would be equally applicable in both cases—No man can do these miracles, or utter these words, except God be with him. If the one is the vindication of his omnipotent power, the other is the proof of his infinite wisdom. His works and his words alike declare his glory. The two are constantly interwoven through the whole course of his public ministry; and while they mutually shed light upon each other, they pour their united radiance over his whole person and character as the great Teacher—the only begotten of the Father, full of grace and truth.

From frequent indications given in the evangelical history, it would seem that the astonishment everywhere produced upon the multitude by his mighty works, was but the counterpart of the profound and universal admiration inspired by his wonderful instructions and manner of teaching. "The common people heard him gladly." "They were astonished at his doctrine, for he taught them as one having authority and not as the Scribes." "About the midst of the feast, Jesus went up into the temple and taught, and the Jews marvelled, saying, How knoweth this man letters, having never learned?" "All bare him witness and wondered at the gracious words which proceeded out of his mouth." Such are the terms in which the impression of his teaching on the public mind is described. And so we find the multitudes following him, with unabated interest, through his whole public career, not more to behold his mighty works than to listen to his matchless instructions. Well, indeed, they might; for, though, as in the case of his miracles, we have only some of the more striking examples of his public discourses recorded, still we have enough to show, that as a teacher he stood alone among men—unique and original both in the form and substance of his teaching.

If we look through the record of his discourses, as reported by three of the evangelists, the first and most obvious characteristic we meet with, is the peculiar form in which he taught the people and his disciples. It was in parables. It is true that parables had been used before to some extent. We find traces of them in the symbolical and highly figurative language of the Old Testament prophets. But no teacher had ever used them to such a degree, or given them such power and beauty as our Saviour.

And none has ever equalled them since. As a vehicle of the most exalted spiritual instruction—as a channel of conveying to the mind of man the deep things of God's kingdom, our Saviour's parables stand without a parallel in the literature of the world. And this is the more remarkable because the parable was a favourite form of instruction with all the Oriental ancient nations. Of course he did not confine himself to parables. Indeed, he seems, at the opening of his ministry, not to have used them at all, as we find him speaking to the people in parables for the first time, from a vessel on the sea of Tiberias. John has not given any of the parables, though he has reported some of his longest and most beautiful discourses. We know, then, that there were occasions, such as the sermon on the mount, and the farewell discourse of the last supper, when he used no parable. Still, after all these exceptions, it remains a striking feature in the public teaching of our Lord, that he spake in parables. The parables which have been reported at length in the first three Evangelists are the following, as arranged by Trench—The Sower, The Tares, The Mustard Seed, The Leaven, The Hid Treasure, The Pearl, The Draw Net, The Unmerciful Servant, The Labourers in the Vineyard, The Two Sons, The Wicked Husbandmen, The Marriage of the King's Son, The Ten Virgins, The Talents, The Seed Growing Secretly, The Two Debtors, The Good Samaritan, The Friend at Midnight, The

Rich Fool, The Barren Fig Tree, The Great Supper, The Lost Sheep, The Lost Piece of Money, The Prodigal Son, The Unjust Steward, The Rich Man and Lazarus, The Unprofitable Servants, The Unjust Judge, The Pharisee and Publican, The Pounds. Besides these thirty regular parables, his discourses are everywhere enlivened with the most striking similes and analogies drawn from the material world around; and, in some instances, we have the higher forms of allegory, as in John's Gospel, where he represents himself as the Good Shepherd, the True Vine, the Bread of Life, the Living Water.

Such was the outward form of his instructions. But there are far more wonderful things in his teaching than this. "Never man spake like this man,"was the report of the commissioned officers of the great Sanhedrim, when they went back as they came, and assigned the reasons why they had not brought him as a prisoner. Men clothed with the authority of the law, are not accustomed to be diverted from the execution of their orders, by the mere words of a peaceable, unarmed citizen. But here are public officers, sent expressly to arrest him, and returning without him, not because of the crowd which surrounded him, or any manifestation of his miraculous power, but solely on account of the words of wisdom which he had uttered in their hearing. There was no other reason to give, and they were not ashamed to give this, extraordinary as it was. How profound must have been their conviction of his superhuman character, that they could go back to their masters with such a plea as this—"Never man spake like this man." Undoubtedly there is to us now, after the conflicts of eighteen centuries, a far deeper import in these words than the awe-struck hearers of our Saviour, who first uttered them, were ever conscious of. The lapse of ages, by the very failure to produce a parallel, has but deepened the impression, that no man ever taught as Jesus. If this was true of him, as compared with all the teachers that these Jewish officers had ever seen, or heard, or read of in their day, it is not less true of him now, as compared with all the men of every age and nation, who have appeared in human history.

It is worthy of note that many of the highest tributes of praise ever bestowed on the character of Jesus, both in sacred and profane history, have been reluctantly wrung from his enemies. Witness that of the devils, whom he had come to dispossess—"I know thee, who thou art, the Holy One of God." Witness that of the unrighteous judge who condemned him to death—"I am innocent of the blood of this just person. Take ye him and crucify him, for I find no fault in him." Witness that of Pilate's wife—"Have thou nothing to do with that just man," and that of Judas—"I have sinned in that I have betrayed innocent blood." Witness that of the Roman centurion at his execution—"Truly this man was the Son of God," and that in the celebrated Confessions of Rousseau—"If the life and death of Socrates were those of a sage, the life and death of Jesus are those of a God." But all things considered, we do not know that either of these remarkable testimonies is any more striking than this confession of the Jewish police at the bar of the Sanhedrim—"Never man spake like this man." They had found him where he was wont to be, in the courts of the temple, on the last great day of the Feast of Tabernacles, surrounded by the ten thousands of Israel, and proclaiming the way of salvation and eternal life to dying men in words of grace and wisdom, such as Jerusalem had never heard before. They listen with the multitude; they are filled with awe; their own hearts respond to the truth of this message from God, for they too are dying sinners; and, instead of laying violent hands on the preacher, they return to attest his Divine mission.

And now while our own hearts in willing and adoring homage respond to this eulogium of the great Teacher, let us ponder what it is in his instructions that so separated him from all other teachers, and made him speak as never man spake.

The first is the subject matter of his discourses. None before his day had ever spoken as he did, and few, indeed, had ever spoken at all on those grand themes which, from first to last, formed the staple of all his public and private instructions. Multitudes of men had in all ages of the world spoken more; and it may be on a greater variety of subjects. Aristotle had among the Greeks, and Cicero among the Romans. But they had spoken mainly of the things of this life; their grandest themes were confined to the present world. On the great things of God and eternity; of life, death, and a judgment to come; of heaven and hell, holiness and sin; of the human soul in its wants and woes, its origin and destiny, its sense of guilt, its fear of retribution, and its longings after immortality; of the deep wretchedness and ruin of our race, and the method of its redemption and recovery—in fact, on all those things relating to God and man, which the human heart is most concerned to know, Jesus spoke with a freedom and a fulness, possible only to a teacher come from God. On such themes as the mysteries of Divine grace, the essential attributes of the Godhead, the doctrines of creation, providence, and redemption, of man's true relation to God and the universe, of the way of salvation from sin, the resurrection of the dead, the church and kingdom of God in the world; and, indeed, on all those grand inspiring themes which now for eighteen centuries have employed the highest intellect of civilized nations, Jesus spoke as never man had spoken. He brought life and immortality to light in the gospel. On all these things, where the uninspired genius of all antiquity, Roman, Grecian, Egyptian, and Chaldean, had groped in utter darkness, he was able to utter heaven's clearest oracles, saying, "We speak that we do know and testify that we have seen." These things are all so familiar to our minds, that we can scarcely appreciate the condition of the world before they were known or even conceived of. But independently of the truth of his doctrines on all these grand mysteries, it is perfectly manifest that he filled the world with new conceptions of them. Except just so far as they had been revealed to holy men of old, who spake as they were moved by the Holy Ghost in the Old Testament Scriptures, they were utterly hidden from the human mind. The patriarchs had looked forward, by faith, and caught some distant glimpses of Immanuel's glory in the latter days, and the prophets had testified beforehand of these wonderful doctrines of his gospel; but outside of the Bible, it was true, for four thousand years, that never man spake like this man touching these great things of God.

Nor is this all. It was much, in a brief career of some three years' labour, to have opened a new world to the thoughts of men. It was much to have added more to the stock of human ideas than all the philosophers of antiquity put together had ever done. It was much to have advanced the revelations of God to a degree of fulness and glory, far beyond anything they had attained under the accumulated light of all the prophets. And it was much to have given the human mind, on themes like these, an impulse which shall but deepen and widen to the end of time. But, perhaps the most remarkable feature of the case is, that he so taught all these exalted doctrines that the world with all its progress of science, and all its advancing intellect, has never been able to add anything to them since his day. Great and marvellous as have been the discoveries of science, and the accessions of knowledge in every field of the heavens and earth, since Jesus dwelt with men; they all together have not added one jot or tittle to those great spiritual and eternal truths which Jesus taught. On all these high and awful mysteries of God and man, and the universe in which we dwell, the world stands to-day with just that stock of knowledge which he left it, and no more, except just so far as his inspired apostles have developed and recorded his instructions in the New Testament. After all our laudations about the dignity of human nature, the advancement of learning, the spirit of bold adventure, of daring experiment, and of profound research, we stand, to-day, in the middle of the nineteenth century, precisely at the point where our race stood when the incarnate Son of God proclaimed the truth—"No man hath seen God at any time; the only begotten Son, who is in the bosom of the Father, he hath declared him." We know from him the true worth and dignity of the soul, its fearful ruin and the price of its redemption; we know from him the way to heaven, the forgiveness of sin, the life everlasting; we know from him that

God is a Spirit, and they that worship him must worship him in spirit and in truth. We know from him that God is a Spirit, infinite, eternal, and unchangeable in his being, wisdom, power, holiness, justice, goodness, and truth; and that to see his face in peace, so as to glorify and enjoy him for ever, we too must be holy—repenting of all our sins and believing on the Son of God for salvation. This is the sum of all the instructions of Jesus, as a Teacher come from God. And, as for anything we can learn from all the teachers of this world besides, God would be as much "the unknown God" to us today, as he was to the Athenians when Paul preached on Mars Hill.

The next remarkable element in our Saviour's teaching, separating him from all others, was the tone of superhuman authority with which he spoke. His peculiar manner of discourse was in perfect harmony with its weighty and solemn matter. One great secret of attraction in his preaching to the astonished and admiring multitudes who crowded to hear him, was that he taught them as one having authority and not as the scribes. He clothes his thoughts in the most attractive form of human speech. His subjects were the most important that ever challenged the attention of men. And he uttered his sayings with the absolute assurance and authority of a message direct from God: "Verily, verily I say unto you." "We speak that we do know, and testify that we have seen"—such was the habitual prelude of personal authority which took the place of that deferential appeal to a higher power with which the ancient prophets had always come, saying, "Thus saith the Lord."

The common people were tired of the hypocrisy and cant of all their learned and professed expounders of the law. They had indeed made void the law by their endless traditions, and laid burdens upon men too grievous to be borne. The whole world was in fact sick at heart for something it knew not what, but something better than it had yet seen. Both Jew and Gentile were weary and worn out, with the ceaseless jargon of the schools and systems of philosophy falsely so called by which men, then as now, darkened counsel by words without knowledge. Here was a new and different teacher, whose words were Yea and Amen; whose words came fresh from the heart, and went directly home to the heart. Here was one who spake as the very oracle and mouthpiece of God. It mattered not where was his temple, or who were his auditors, it was always the same voice of absolute certainty and of Divine power. In the crowded synagogue, or the still more crowded wayside, on the mountain's brow or on the seashore, in distant desert places, or at the great national gatherings of the people, in the domestic circle of affection at Bethany, or amid the public courts of the temple where he rebuked the pride of chief priest, scribe, and Pharisee, it was always the same tone of infallible certainty, and of undisputed supremacy. It was more than the return of the spirit and power of Elijah. It was one, who while stooping to men of low estate and even unto babes, yet ever spake with the graceful majesty of a king, and the conscious authority of God manifest in the flesh.

There are three different classes of circumstances in the life of our Lord, wherein we find him speaking with this tone of superhuman authority.

The first embraces all those occasions in which he wrought his mighty works. These cannot be numbered. But as above stated we have thirty or more of them, circumstantially narrated, when by a single word of power, he spake and it was done, he commanded and it stood fast. We refer not now to the miracle itself, but to the authoritative tone of him who speaks it into being. It is precisely the manner of Him who at the beginning said, "Let there be light, and there was light." The eyewitnesses themselves were everywhere struck with this tone of supremacy and command in Jesus, "What manner of man is this? For he commandeth even the winds and water, and they obey him." "They were all amazed, and spake among themselves, saying, What a word is this? For with authority and power he commandeth the unclean spirits, and they obey him." Here indeed lies the striking difference between his miracles and all those of the prophets on the one hand, his apostles on the other—that his are all performed in virtue of his own inherent power, without the intervention of other means or agencies. "I will," says he, "be thou clean." "Take up thy bed and walk." "Stretch forth thine hand: and he stretched it forth whole as the other." "Daughter, thy sins be forgiven thee: go in peace." "Damsel, I say unto thee, Arise." "Lazarus, come forth;" and he that was dead came forth, bound hand and foot. Such was our Saviour's manner of performing his mighty works. And on all these occasions he spake as man never spake.

The second class embraces all the occasions on which he delivered his formal and public discourses in the presence of his disciples and the multitudes of the Jewish people. Of these we have remarkable examples in the sermon on the mount, in his description of the last judgment in the 25th chapter of Matthew, in his invective against the scribes and Pharisees in the twenty-third, in the various discourses in the temple at the great Jewish festivals, as recorded by John, and in his farewell discourse to his disciples alone, on the night before he suffered. No man can listen to these solemn revelations of things unseen and eternal—things on which no mortal tongue had ever ventured to speak thus before—without feeling their awful and unapproachable sublimity. Especially is this the case with his last discourses, when we know that their author, so far as he was a man at all, was but a young man in the prime of life, expecting voluntarily to lay down his life on the morrow for the truth of his convictions. Socrates, under somewhat similar circumstances, has been an object of the world's admiration. But mere admiration is far short of the merits of this case. No man can read and ponder the words of Jesus, without the conviction that their author stood in an attitude of moral power and superiority over all the men of this world, such as nothing could inspire less than the consciousness that he was either a teacher come from God, or God himself.

But if he was the one, he was the other. If he was the less, then he was of necessity the greater. It is a case in which the less involves and draws after it the whole truth of the greater proposition. If he was a teacher come from God, as it is impossible to deny he was, then he was God himself, because he expressly claimed to be God, and died asserting the claim. A teacher come from God, whose whole life and actions had been what his were, could not have spoken anything but the truth. But one of the great truths which he never ceased to speak, through his whole public career to the very tribunal which condemned him to death, was that he was the Son of God, that he was equal with God, that he was God. So that if the miracles and the words of Jesus force us to the alternative that he was either a teacher from God, or God manifest in the flesh, that alternative shuts us up to but one conclusion—that he was all that he claimed to be. And now to feel in your inmost heart, that this is the true and only possible alternative, listen to some of those words which no man before or since ever spake of himself: "Heaven and earth shall pass away, but my words shall not pass away. Not every one that saith unto me, Lord, Lord, shall enter into the kingdom of heaven; but he that doeth the will of my Father which is in heaven. Father, glorify thou me with thine own self with the glory which I had with thee before the world was. Then shall ye see the Son of Man coming in the clouds of heaven. He shall sit upon the throne of his glory, and before him all nations shall be gathered; and he shall separate them one from another, as a shepherd divideth his sheep from the goats. All power is given to me in heaven and earth. Go ye, therefore, and teach all nations, baptizing them in the name of the Father, and of the Son, and of the Holy Ghost. Lo, I am with you always, even to the end of the world. He that believeth and is baptized shall be saved, and he that believeth not shall be damned."

When did mortal man ever speak thus? How would such language have sounded on the lips of Abraham, or Moses, or Daniel, or Paul? Men in their folly have sometimes talked of Jesus as a mere man. But, leaving out of view his miracles, and taking only his words, the difference between him and every other man is an infinite difference. If ever there was a mortal disposed to speak in a tone of authority, and arrogate to himself all human powers, it was that mighty conqueror, whose edicts gave law to Europe and whose sword had overturned her thrones. But Napoleon never spake like this. Even at the meridian height of his pomp and power, words like these, or anything approaching them, would have convicted him in the sight of the universe of being either a blasphemer or insane. And with reverence be it spoken, there is nothing that could exempt the mere humanity of Jesus from the same charge. It is only because he is God over all, blessed for ever, that these awful and superhuman words are the words of soberness and truth.

The third class of occasions on which he showed the same superhuman wisdom, embraces all his private informal interviews and conversations—occasions when he wrought no mighty works, and delivered no public discourses, but appeared most like a man. Witness that, for example, with Nathaniel in the first chapter of John, and that with Nicodemus in the third. Witness the interview with the young ruler, and the one with the lawyer who tempted him. See how he puts to silence, in succession, the wily deputations from the Herodians, the Sadducees, and the Pharisees, till no man durst ask him any more questions. See him alone before the judgment-seat of Pilate—the arrogant Roman evidently awed into admiration and fear by the silent and sublime demeanour of his suffering prisoner! To my own mind, there is scarcely anything in the New Testament more remarkable and significant than this—that Jesus Christ, through all those scenes of humiliation, suffering, and the daily intercourse of life, in which it was necessary for him to appear most like a man and least like a God, should yet so speak and act as to make men feel that he was more than man. From the hour in which he stood in the midst of the doctors of the temple at the age of twelve, down to that in which he stood before his last accusers, and his final judge, there was something about him—in his every word, look, and action—which made every one who came in contact with him, feel that he was a superior being.

When we mark that calm, quiet, self-possessed, and yet authoritative tone in which he accosted both friends and foes, that gentle yet uncompromising dignity and sense of superiority which pervaded his every instruction to man, woman, or child; when we follow him to the retreats of private life in the presence of his disciples alone, or in the bosom of the loved family at Bethany; when in these familiar and unstudied moments we hear him say, "My meat is to do the will of him that sent me and to finish his work. For I came down from heaven not to do mine own will, but the will of Him that sent me;" when we hear him saying to the sorrowing sister of Lazarus, "I am the resurrection and the life; he that believeth in me, though he were dead yet shall he live; and he that liveth, and believeth in me shall never die;" when we follow him to the place of death, and hear him answer the last request of one who languished at his side, "This day shalt thou be with me in paradise," we are constrained to feel, that never man spake like this man. We bear testimony with Nathaniel, "Rabbi, thou art the Son of God, thou art the king of Israel." For not only does he speak of things men never knew before, and never could have known; but, unlike all the teachers of antiquity, who rested their instructions on a foregoing authority higher than their own, he speaks, as one having absolute, inherent, personal, and underived knowledge of all things whereof he affirms. His teaching, like his power, is wholly independent of man.

CHAPTER VI.

HIS IMMACULATE VIRTUES.

Nothing, perhaps, has ever made a deeper impression upon the heart of the world than the compassion of Jesus. It is a quality which all men, even the unregenerate, have been ready to acknowledge and admire, when, perhaps, they could see no other beauty in Immanuel. Mercy, compassion, sympathy with the deep woes of man, strikes a chord in every human bosom, that is not utterly dead to all the higher and better instincts of our fallen nature. Orators praise it. Poets celebrate it in their loftiest strains. Good men love and practise it. Bad men do homage to it, as the sum of all goodness. The man who is ready to risk his life to save others, whose bosom melts with pity for the poor, whose generous sympathies respond to every cry of human anguish, wins not only the approval of all the good, but even the plaudits of those who are destitute of the attribute they extol. The heart of man was made to be moved by sympathy. It needs the sympathies both of God and men. There is scarcely anything which it needs more. It cannot stand alone. It needs something to lean upon.

And hence, whenever a true hearted Howard appears, braving danger and death, out of that yearning love which he bears towards the perishing, all men are ready to take him to their hearts, not only as a brother but as a very idol. This deep and universal sentiment of admiration for philanthropy is vividly depicted, though with an approach to extravagance, in the lines:

> "The spirits of the just,
> When first arrayed in Virtue's purest robe,
> They saw her Howard traversing the globe,
> Mistook a mortal for an angel guest,
> And asked what seraph's foot the earth imprest.
> Onward he flies—disease and death retire,
> And wondering demons hate him and admire.

If such a character as Howard's, and such a life of self-sacrificing good will, may win a world's approval—call down encomium from heaven, and extort reluctant homage from the lost—what ought to be our appreciation of the virtues human and Divine that dwelt in the bosom of Jesus? If we could for a moment divest ourselves of the peculiar relations in which we stand to him as a Saviour and a God, and then look upon him simply as a fellow-man, as we look upon Howard, it is clear that we should even then behold in him an example of generous, heroic, and self-sacrificing virtue, which has no parallel in the annals of mankind. Even on the score of philanthropy and brotherhood it has no parallel among men. It was a philanthropy embracing first the objects of love immediately surrounding him—his disciples—and then all his countrymen, and then all the world. It was a philanthropy that went down to the abodes of poverty, of disease, of want, and held familiar converse with all its woes. It was a Divine compassion that sought to save the lost, the vile, the outcast; that could eat with publicans and sinners, when such companionship was not regarded as a virtue. It was a compassion which, while grasping the wide world, did not overlook even the babes and sucklings that clustered at its feet. The Son of man came not to be ministered unto, but to minister, and to give his life a ransom for others. He came to seek and to save that which was lost; not only the lost sheep of the house of Israel, but the lost of all nations and generations of men. For our sakes he became poor. As before remarked, there is no theme on which the sacred writers dwell with greater delight and wonder than this infinite compassion of Immanuel—this condescension to the poor—this emptying himself of his Divine glory, that he might come to our relief—might bear our griefs and carry our sorrows—might become our brother, touched with our infirmities, tempted in all points like as we are, yet without sin. It is the burden of the prophet's vision. It inspires the song of the sweet psalmist of Israel. It is the story of all the evangelists. It is the meditation of all the apostles, as they carry the glad tidings to the end of the earth: "Ye know the grace of our Lord

Jesus Christ, that whereas he was rich, yet for our sakes he became poor, that we through his poverty might be rich."

> "Aside the Prince of glory threw
> His most Divine array,
> And wrapped his Godhead in a veil
> Of our inferior clay."

"And being found in fashion as a man, he humbled himself, and became obedient unto death, even the death of the cross." His whole public life, from his baptism to the great expiation on Calvary, was a life of sympathy with the suffering, and of merciful visitation to the poor. Though he was a man of sorrows, as bearing the sins of the whole world—bearing them onward to the scene of final sacrifice—and though he had not where to lay his head in the world he had created, and was now about to redeem—yet was he never known to turn away from a single sinner however humble, and however vile, of all the ten thousands that sought his favour.

It has often been noticed how the character of Immanuel is illustrated in his life. The sacred writers describe his virtues by simply narrating his actions. They set before us a succession of the most touching and graphic scenes, which, far better than any words of eulogy, display his benevolent compassions, and the full glory of his human and Divine perfection. As his mission was to preach the gospel to the poor, to seek the lost sheep of the house of Israel, to humble himself to the ministry of a servant; so of necessity, philanthropy, benevolence, compassion, becomes the prominent attribute in this whole manifestation of his character. It is in the human life of Jesus, more than in anything else, that we behold the love of God. The only begotten Son, who was in the bosom of the Father. came into the world, and led a life of compassion, not only that he might save us, but that he might thus reveal the love of God. Hence we find all his mighty works partaking of this element of compassion—wrought for the deliverance of the wretched and the outcast, or of the humble and helpless. The very titles of his acts of mercy are enough to illustrate his character; and the great masters of art have found no higher study than to reproduce the scene. Thus we have, Christ healing the Sick, Christ blessing little Children, Christ feeding the Multitudes, Christ raising the Widow's Son, Christ restoring Lazarus, Christ weeping over Jerusalem. In all these and other similar scenes that make up the history of his life, the grand distinguishing attribute is mercy. It is the crowning glory of his manhood. It is the bright effulgence of that Godhead, which shines out through the veil of this human tabernacle. Nothing could be more appropriate than such a manifestation of celestial virtue. If we had been told beforehand that God would manifest himself in the form of a man; that celestial Divine virtue would become incarnate and display all its brightest glories in a living, human character; and that such a revelation was to be made for the benefit, and amid all the sufferings, of our wretched, dying race, it would be the dictate of reason, that God, thus manifesting himself, should clothe himself with all those attributes of condescension, sympathy, compassion, and love, which we now behold in the person of Immanuel. This is precisely the form of virtue which such a manifestation, for such a purpose, and in such a world, would demand. Nor can we conceive of anything that could be taken away from the character of Jesus Christ, on the one hand, nor of a single attribute that could be added to it on the other, that would make its adaptation more complete, and its beauty more symmetrical and glorious. One shade more, one ray less, would have marred that absolute perfection which now adorns his character. More of the Divine and less of the human; more of majesty and less of condescension; greater displays of power and fewer deeds of love, instead of lending new attractions to the cross, would have only detracted from that matchless power and pathos by which it now draws all men unto it.

There is nothing in the life of Jesus more significant of his immaculate virtue, and more in keeping with all the ends for which such virtue became incarnate, than his tears. When we consider who he was, and why he came into the world, his tears are as indicative of his Divine mission and as precious to us, as his mighty works. They are the tokens of his unspeakable love. They are the seals of a sympathy in our sorrows, such as, without them, we did not know God could feel for sinners. They are the proofs of an interest in our welfare which assures our fainting hearts, that He, who has undertaken for us, is as willing as he is able to save. And it is striking to notice through the sacred narrative, how the tears of Jesus flow mingling with his mighty works. It was at the grave of Lazarus, and when in a few moments the sleep of death was to be broken by a word of omnipotence, that Jesus wept. The very scene which calls forth the sublimest attributes of the Godhead—the scene of his almighty triumph over death and the grave—is that in which all the tenderest sympathies of his immaculate human heart are touched, and find appropriate utterance in tears. If the war-worn conqueror of a hundred battles should be seen to weep in the moment of his greatest victory, it would be but a faint approach to that power of emotion which filled the Son of God with tears at the grave of Lazarus. "Jesus wept." And those around, filled with admiration and awe, that one who had been known to give sight to the blind, should thus weep, said, Behold how he loved him! Could not this man, endowed with such power, and moved by such love, had he been here, have caused that Lazarus should not have died? The mighty men of this world, in the height of their power, are not accustomed to weep at the sight of others' woe. But Jesus wept, even in that sublime hour, when he burst asunder the bands of death—wept responsive to the tears of those bereaved and sorrowing sisters who were imploring his help—wept in deep and yearning sympathy with all the sufferings and desolation which this much-loved family had endured in the loss of a brother—wept out of his full and unutterable love for that poor dying human nature, whose countless griefs he had come to bear, whose dreadful maladies he had come to heal. Oh! it was fit that the Man of sorrows should thus weep. Though he was the Prince of glory, the Conqueror of death and hell, it was fit that the Friend of sinners should weep at the grave. Though he could say to the stricken hearts around him, Thy brother shall rise again; and, though he did say, with Divine power, ere those tears of love were dry upon his cheek, "Lazarus, come forth," still nothing could be more in keeping with the great work he came to do, than that he should weep at the grave. For all flesh weeps there. Every human being weeps there, even if he weeps no where else. There is no man so hard as not to weep for his dead. And there is no man so wicked or worthless as not to have the tribute of a tear when he is gone. It is one of the saddest, but one of the most inalienable portions of our earthly heritage, that we are all, sooner or later, called to weep over our dead. How significant and appropriate to the character of our great

Mediator, who came to rescue us from the grasp of sin and death, that we should have this simple and touching memorial of his love—JESUS WEPT!

But this is not the only record of his tenderness. We read of another memorable occasion which called forth the tears of the Son of God. It was his last visit to Jerusalem—that which led him, as he had so often told his disciples, to go up for the express purpose of dying there. It was on the day of his public and triumphal entry into the holy city, according to that ancient prophecy which had described, in joyful strains, Zion's king as coming to her with salvation, riding upon the foal of an ass. It was an occasion which, occurring only a few days before the great annual feast of the Passover, had drawn together an unwonted number of his friends and followers, as well as a vast concourse of the people, who had beheld his mighty works in Galilee, or had still more recently been the witnesses of his great miracle near Jerusalem, the resurrection of Lazarus. Leaving Bethany, where he had but lately wrought this mighty work, and accompanied by the vast multitudes, both of those who had followed him, and of those who had come out of the city to welcome his approach, he passed over the Mount of Olives, and came at once within full view of that glorious city.

He had not seen it before for more than three months. He had left it at the feast of the Dedication, a voluntary exile, because his hour had not then come to die. He had at that time bidden it farewell in the following sorrowful words, recorded by Luke: "O Jerusalem! Jerusalem! which killest the prophets and stonest them that are sent unto thee, how often would I have gathered thy children together as a hen doth gather her brood under her wings, but ye would not! Behold your house is left unto you desolate. And verily I say unto you, Ye shall not see me until the time come when ye shall say, Blessed is he that cometh in the name of the Lord."

And now that time had come. He was approaching, to leave Jerusalem no more, till he should have laid down his life as a sacrifice for the sins of the world. "For," said he, "it cannot be that a prophet perish out of Jerusalem." He was coming in the name of the Lord to die, whilst a joyful multitude, thinking he was coming to set up his temporal kingdom on the throne of David, strewed their garments and palm branches in his way, and cried aloud: "Hosanna! Blessed be the King of Israel, that cometh in the name of the Lord. Peace in heaven, and glory in the highest."

From the point of descent of the Mount of Olives, over which he was now passing, in a direction directly west and across the deep valley of Jehoshaphat, appeared the city in all its ancient grandeur. He had at one view the whole outline of its eastern wall surmounting the brow of the hill, and rising some two hundre l feet above the valley;

and above and beyond that, the gorgeous temple, covering the whole summit of Mount Moriah, with its beautiful eastern gate, its white marble walls, its alabaster porticoes and colonnades, its gold-covered pinnacles and turrets—all flashing back the morning light, and sparkling like "a mountain of snow studded with jewels." On that glorious spectacle, the pilgrims of every generation had fixed their eyes with devout and admiring wonder, even from the days of Solomon. Can we doubt that the Son of God now paused to gaze upon such a scene of loveliness?

"There stood Jerusalem. How fair she looked,
The silver sun on all her palaces,
And her fair daughters 'mid the golden spires,
Tending their terrace flowers, and Kedron's stream
Lacing the meadows with its silver band,
And breathing its mist mantle on the sky
With the morn's exhalations. There she stood,
Jerusalem, the city of his love,
Chosen from all the earth; Jerusalem,
That knew him not, and had rejected him;
Jerusalem for whom he came to die."

And how was Jesus affected by all this scene of external magnificence—the chosen seat of God's favoured covenant people? He wept over it. He mingled his tears of pity with prophetic warnings of its approach ng doom. The sacred writer tells us that "when he was come near he beheld the city and wept over it, saying, If thou hadst known, even thou, at least, in this thy day, the things which belong unto thy peace! But now they are hid from thine eyes. For the days shall come upon thee, that thine enemies shall cast a trench about thee, and compass thee round, and keep thee in on every side, and shall lay thee even with the ground, and thy children within thee; and they shall not leave in thee one stone upon another; because thou knewest not the time of thy visitation."

Here again, as in so many other instances, we behold the mysterious blending of all his Divine and human attributes. While all the deep fountains of Divine and human love are moved within him; while the warm tears of humanity stream from his eyes, as he thinks of the hapless fate of the incorrigible but beloved city, with all the consciousness of Divine power, and with a perfect foresight of all the sad future, he pronounces its terrible doom. And what a contrast between this deep and solitary sorrow of the Son of God, and the enthusiastic joy of the multitude which surrounds him! How utterly unlike every other king and conqueror in the world's history, when borne along in triumphal procession, amid the shouts and hosannas of an applauding and rejoicing people! "And when he was come nigh, even now at the descent of the Mount of Olives, the whole multitude of the disciples began to rejoice and praise God, with a loud voice, for all the mighty works they had seen."

But Jesus wept—wept alone: for, at that moment of universal joy around him, there was probably not one human heart in all the throng that could understand or appreciate his sorrow. He wept not for himself, but for others; not on account of the sufferings he was so soon to endure, but on account of the woes of the doomed city, and of this guilty world. He wept for the city and the people he had come to save; whom he would have died to save; to whom he had so long preached, and for whom he had so often prayed. And now he saw that the day of merciful visitation was closing for ever. He came unto his own and his own had not received him. The harvest was passed; the summer was ended; and the sinners of Jerusalem, as if about to forestall the doom of all sinners to the end of time, were not saved.

"He thought not of the death that he should die,
He thought not of the thorns he knew must pierce
His forehead—of the buffet on the cheek—
The scourge—the mocking homage—the foul scorn.
Gethsemane stood out beneath his eye,
Clear in the morning sun. And Golgotha
Stood bare and desert by the city wall.
And in its midst to his prophetic eye
Rose the rough cross, and its keen agonies,
The nails, the spear, and the insulting sponge,
The blood and water gushing from his side.
Aye! he forgot all this. He only saw
Jerusalem, the chosen, the loved, the lost;
He only felt, that for her sake his life
Was vainly given; and in his pitying love,
The sufferings, that would clothe the heavens in black
Were quite forgotten. Was there ever love
In earth or heaven like this?"

But we pause. Human language is inadequate to delineate the character of Immanuel, even in one of its virtues. The inspired writers have recorded for us his words, breathing the love of heaven; they have told us of his tears, the outward symbols of that love; and then they have set before us the amazing scene of his death, as its highest conceivable proof and manifestation. Our object has been to single out this unparalleled love simply as an illustration of the manifold virtues or attributes, that shone forth, in full-orbed perfection, from the whole Divine and human nature of Jesus. We have taken this one perfection, because from the nature of the case, it had to bear a prominent part in his estate of humiliation, and his ministry of mercy in our suffering world; and also because it is one which is of the very essence of the gospel which he preached, and of the God whom he came to reveal. Love is the fulfilling of every law of the gospel; and God himself is love. The perfect love of Jesus may, therefore, be taken as the crowning proof and seal of all his other virtues. It was impossible that there should be such a manifestation of all Divine and human sympathies even unto death, without at the same time carrying with it the full play of every other conceivable perfection.

Hence we find exhibited in the life of Jesus all other virtues—not only an absolute sinless humanity, but a humanity completely radiant with every positive excellence which can be conceived of, as belonging to an incarnate Deity. We behold at every step the character of one who, though living among sinners, and at last dying for sinners, and tempted in all points like as we are, was yet holy, harmless, undefiled, and separate from sinners. We behold not only kindness, courtesy, condescension, sympathy, moderation, gentleness, self-denial, patience, fortitude, and all those qualities that adorn the relationships of human life; but we behold all the higher and nobler attributes of virtue—an inflexible justice, an unflinching courage, an undeviating truthfulness, a steadfast purpose, an uncompromising honour, a genuine devotion, a heroic faith, a self-sacrificing zeal, a sublime energy, and an immaculate holiness, such as, even aside from his boundless love, never met before in any human character. Each trait was absolutely perfect in itself, and absolutely perfect in its combination with all the rest. Such a character of moral excellence is without a parallel in the annals of mankind. And such a character in such a world as this, is a demonstration complete that its possessor was Divine.

CHAPTER VII.

THE MANIFESTATIONS OF HIS GLORY.

In reading the life of our blessed Lord, we must not forget that there were reasons which made it necessary that his celestial beauty and all his Divine attributes should be partially concealed from men during the whole period of his incarnation. The work he came into the world to accomplish was essentially a work of suffering and death. His condition while performing that work was of necessity one of deep humiliation, inconsistent with any general and overpowering display of Divine glory. It was the sun in a state of eclipse. Though he was, even while dwelling in mortal clay, the brightness of the Father's glory and the express image of his person, possessing all the fulness of the Godhead bodily, yet that glory was under a cloud, hidden, not only from the world, but, in great measure, from his most intimate friends and disciples. In view of this low estate we find Isaiah foretelling that he would be despised and rejected of men, an object of astonishment and offence to many, because his visage was so marred more than any man, and his form more than the sons of men.

"For he shall grow up before him as a tender plant, and as a root out of a dry ground; he hath no form nor comeliness; and when we shall see him there is no beauty that we should desire him."

But, notwithstanding this deep humiliation and hiding of his power, we find, both in Isaiah and other prophets, indications that even in the days of his flesh, there should break forth many signal displays of his Divine glory and beauty. The sun must, indeed, be hidden, but it was not to be a total eclipse. Isaiah speaks of him as "the Branch of the Lord, beautiful and glorious;" "Thine eyes shall see the King in his beauty," and David, drawing aside that veil of suffering which so concealed his glory from mortal view, exclaims, "Thy people shall be willing in the day of thy power; in the beauties of holiness from the womb of the morning, thou hast the dew of thy youth."

Accordingly we find the life of Jesus Christ, as related by the evangelists, everywhere in exact correspondence with this two-fold prophetical representation of his humiliation and his glory. For, while there hangs over his whole mortal career, from the manger to the cross, that eclipse of Divine glories which so well befitted a suffering Messiah, there were not wanting, even at the darkest hour, bright glimpses of celestial light, indicating that the darkness must soon pass, and the sun rise again triumphant in his meridian splendor. Over and above all his miracles and mighty works, there were other manifestations of his glory—indications of a supernatural order, given to him from the Father—at once tokens to him of his Father's approving love, and proofs to his disciples that he was the beloved Son of God.

These, from the very nature of the case, had to be given as occasional manifestations, or exceptions from the general tenor of our Saviour's life. For it is obvious that, had they occurred so frequently as to become the rule, and not the exception, during his incarnation, they must have defeated the great work of suffering and death, which could be performed only in an estate of humiliation. And so we find that, unlike all the ordinary transactions and events of his life, these occasional manifestations of supernatural power and glory were, for the most part, witnessed by but a few chosen spectators. When he suffered and died, the world looked on the spectacle. Thousands of human eyes gazed on the helpless sufferer. But no man saw him rise from the dead. That glory was reserved for the angels alone. All his appearances after his resurrection, during the forty days preceding his ascension, as belonging, properly, to his estate of exaltation, took place in the presence of his disciples alone, varying in number from one to above five hundred. That last and most glorious act of all, when he ascended up on high, must have been witnessed by a comparatively small number. And so all the brightest manifestations of his glory, prior to his resurrection, were not given to the world at large, but to a few spectators. When an angel was sent from heaven to announce his advent, and that of his forerunner, in the one case Zacharias, and in the other Mary, were the sole recipients of the message. When at his birth a multitude of angels sang Glory to God in the highest; peace on earth, good will to men, a few shepherds at Bethlehem were all that heard the song. When his star appeared in the east, and hovered over his manger, though many may have seen it, yet none but a few wise men seem to have understood its peculiar glory. When angels descended and ministered to him at the end of his temptations in the wilderness, we are told that he was alone with the wild beasts. No mortal saw his heavenly visitants. In the awful hour of his agony in the garden of Gethsemane, when he had withdrawn from the presence of the disciples to pray alone, there appeared unto him an angel from heaven, strengthening him. But all these signs of power were hidden from the world.

In two instances, recorded by the evangelists, there seem to have been multitudes present to witness these extraordinary manifestations of his glory. The one was at his baptism, when the heavens were opened to him, and he saw the Spirit of God descending like a dove and lighting upon him. And lo, a voice from heaven, saying, This is my beloved Son in whom I am well pleased. The other was on a subsequent occasion, during his last days, in the

8

temple at Jerusalem, when in answer to his prayer, "Father, glorify thy name," there came a voice from heaven, saying, "I have both glorified it, and will glorify it again." We cannot tell what number of people saw and heard these two supernatural manifestations of his glory. But on another still more remarkable occasion, that of his transfiguration on the Mount, we know that only three chosen disciples were present with Moses and Elias, to behold his glory, and that these were charged not to make it known till he should have risen from the dead; thereby showing that this and similar revelations belonged not properly to his mortal life, but to his risen and exalted state.

The transfiguration, which is so fully recorded by three of the evangelists, and referred to by the Apostle Peter in his second epistle, is indeed one of the most wonderful and significant transactions in our Saviour's history, and deserves a special consideration. It may be taken as the type or exponent of all those extraordinary manifestations of his glory, which seem to have been granted from time to time, as a sort of pledge or earnest of the future, in order to relieve the darkness and offset the deep humiliation of his incarnate mortal life. St. Peter evidently lays peculiar stress upon this transfiguration, when, writing long after its occurrence, he says, "We have not followed cunningly devised fables, when we made known unto you the power and coming of our Lord Jesus Christ, but were eye witnesses of his majesty. For he received from God the Father honour and glory, when there came such a voice to him from the excellent glory, "This is my beloved Son in whom I am well pleased. And this voice which came from heaven we heard, when we were with him in the holy Mount." The Apostle John probably refers to this event, when he says, "The Word was made flesh and dwelt among us, and we beheld his glory, the glory as of the only begotten of the Father, full of grace and truth." It is also worthy of notice, that in describing his sublime vision of the Saviour in the opening chapter of the Apocalypse, where he appears in glory as the Alpha and Omega, the First and the Last, this apostle uses language similar to that in which the transfiguration is described: "His head and his hairs were white like wool, as white as snow; and his eyes were as a flame of fire; and his countenance as the sun shining in his strength."

But let us turn to the account of the transfiguration as recorded by Matthew. "After six days Jesus taketh Peter, James, and John his brother, and bringeth them up into a high mountain apart; and was transfigured before them: and his face did shine as the sun, and his raiment was white as the light." Luke adds, that he went up to pray, and that as he prayed, the fashion of his countenance was altered, and his raiment became white and glistening. "And behold, there appeared unto them

Moses and Elias talking with him." Luke again adds the subject of discourse, "who appeared in glory and spake of his decease which he should accomplish at Jerusalem." "Then answered Peter, and said unto Jesus, Lord, it is good for us to be here; if thou wilt, let us make here three tabernacles; one for thee, and one for Moses, and one for Elias:" as Luke adds, not knowing what he said. "While he yet spake, behold a bright cloud overshadowed them; and behold a voice out of the cloud, which said, This is my beloved Son in whom I am well pleased; hear ye him. And when the disciples heard it, they fell on their face, and were sore afraid." Luke says, they feared as they entered into the cloud. "And Jesus came and touched them, and said, Arise, and be not afraid. And when they had lifted up their eyes, they saw no man save Jesus only. And as they came down from the mountain, Jesus charged them, saying, Tell the vision to no man until the Son of man be risen again from the dead." Mark tells us that they kept that saying with themselves, questioning one with another, what the rising from the dead should mean; and he further adds, that all the people, when they beheld him as he came down from the mount, were greatly amazed, and running to him, saluted him. From this it would seem, that, as in the case of Moses on a similar occasion, some vestiges of the excellent glory still lingered about his person, and inspired the multitude with wonder and adoration.

The first thing claiming attention in this account of the transfiguration is the time of its occurrence. It was six days after our Saviour's most emphatic declaration to his disciples that he must suffer death at Jerusalem. In the vicinity of Cæsarea Philippi, while conversing with the disciples about his Messiahship, he had received from Peter that good and strong confession, Thou art the Christ, the Son of the living God, which led him to say, Thou art Peter, and upon this rock I will build my church, and the gates of hell shall not prevail against it. "From that time forth," we are told, "began Jesus to show unto his disciples, how that he must go unto Jerusalem, and suffer many things of the elders and chief priests and scribes, and be killed, and be raised again the third day." This was in the last year of his public ministry, and probably about nine months before his death. As the disciples could neither comprehend the mystery of his resurrection, nor see the necessity for his death, one object of the transfiguration was evidently to impress their minds with the certainty of these great facts. Peter had, ir his ardent zeal, even ventured to rebuke him, foı thus speaking of a speedy and violent death. But he rebukes the disciple in turn, and takes occasion to utter some of the most weighty and fundamental truths of his gospel, saying, as no mortal man had ever said before, "If any man will come after me, let him deny himself and take up his cross and follow me. For whosoever will save his life, shall lose it; and whosoever will lose his life for my sake, shall find it. For what is a man profited, if he shall gain the whole world and lose his own soul? or what shall a man give in exchange for his soul? For the Son of man shall come in the glory of his Father with his angels, and then he shall reward every man according to his works. Verily, I say unto you, There be some standing here, which shall not taste of death, till they see the Son of man coming in his kingdom."

In immediate connection with these sublime utterances, in each of the three evangelists, stands the record of his transfiguration. There can be no doubt, that as a manifestation of his celestial glory, and as a type and symbol of that eternal kingdom of which he had just spoken, and in the full glory of which he should come at the last day, this transfiguration was in his mind as the first and immediate fulfilment of the prediction. "There be some standing here who shall not taste of death till they see the Son of man coming in his kingdom." For this being a demonstration from heaven of his eternal power and Godhead—the very prelude, pledge, and proof of his final and glorious appearing, might well be regarded by those who saw it, as the coming of his kingdom. Indeed we know that the apostle Peter did so regard it; for he says, "We have not followed cunningly devised fables, when we made known unto you the power and coming of our Lord Jesus Christ, but were eyewitnesses of his majesty."

From these and other circumstances attending the transfiguration, it is easy to see what was its great design. To the three disciples who witnessed it, it was evidently intended to be a sublime and prophetic representation of Immanuel in his glory —that glory which he had before he came into the world, which he now wears in heaven, and in which he will come at last to judge the world. It was intended for the confirmation of their faith, and, when the seal of secrecy should be removed, to be a source of instruction and consolation to his church through all ages. To the Saviour himself it probably had another and still higher significance. Like the presence of ministering angels in his hours of trial and agony, and like other celestial attestations, which he received from time to time, it no doubt had the great purpose of sustaining his own faith, and of preparing him for the great sacrifice which he was to make at Jerusalem. The well-beloved Son of God was not to be left entirely alone even in his deep humiliation. He needed, and from time to time, he received these high tokens of the Father's love, and these prelibations of the glory which awaited him when his work should have been accomplished.

It is interesting to notice in this scene the important agency of prayer. One evangelist tells us that he went up into the mount to pray; and that as he prayed the fashion of his countenance was changed. What honour does the Son of God place upon prayer in thus using it in all the great transactions of his life! And what honour does the Father place upon it, in granting all his most glorious manifestations in answer to prayer! At his baptism, it was while he prayed, that the heavens were opened to him, and the Spirit descended upon him, and a voice came from heaven: "This is my beloved Son." It was while he was uttering the language of prayer, that the same voice was heard again in the temple. Before he called Lazarus from the grave, he lifted up his eyes to heaven in thanksgiving and prayer. And so here, it is prayer that opens the heavens on the Mount of transfiguration, and brings down the glorified messengers. If Immanuel found it good to pray, how much more ought sinful, helpless men always to pray and not to faint!

One of the most significant circumstances connected with the vision, was, that Moses and Elias should appear. Of all the saints who had lived under the Old Testament dispensation, and gone to glory, it was most appropriate that these two should be manifested on this occasion—Moses as the great lawgiver of Israel, and Elijah as the most remarkable example and representative of the prophetic order. As Christ is the end of the whole legal system, and the burden of all the prophets; as all the Scriptures, both of the law and the prophets, pointed to his advent; so now the great lawgiver and the great typal prophet, appear to him in glory, and discourse of that death which was to fulfil both the law and the prophets. Indeed, it was predicted of him, that he should be a prophet like unto Moses, and that Elijah should be sent as his immediate forerunner to prepare for his coming. And so, these two great names, the one opening the Scriptures of the law, and the other closing those of the prophets, by this prediction in Malachi, in a manner, represent the whole period of preparation, the four thousand years before Immanuel's advent; and now when the fulness of time had come, they appear on the holy Mount to bear witness and homage to him as Lord of all. The glorified spirit of the prophet, in the same glorified body, which, without tasting death, had once been wafted to heaven in a chariot of fire and horsemen of fire, comes down to the cloud-covered Mount on this new and unusual ministry. And the once disembodied spirit of the great lawgiver, which had been so long in heaven, is now arrayed in a mortal form, prepared for the occasion, or else in that very body, raised from the dead, which the Lord himself had buried in a valley of the land of Moab, where no man knew of his sepulchre. In either case, and in both examples, it was a sublime and glorious demonstration of the great truth of another and higher life for man.

It was an occasion on which the two worlds seemed to meet face to face. Heaven was there, represented by these glorified spirits of just men made perfect, who, for ages, had tasted its bliss. And earth was there, represented by the three apostles in all their frailty, wonderment, and aspiration after better things. Between them stood Immanuel, clothed now in the nature of both, fit Mediator thus between God and man, and only ladder of ascent from the mortal to the immortal. As it was a meeting and commingling of the two worlds, earth and heaven, brief indeed in its duration, but prefiguring one which is to be eternal, so also was it a striking representation of the unity of the church of God, under all forms and dispensations. Here, on a lone mountain summit, apart from every human abode, and hidden from the gaze of other men, the three disciples have an ocular demonstration of Zion's glory in her Great Redeemer. Here is the church of the ancient covenant in the person of two of his greatest teachers; representing all those who by faith and patience had already inherited the promises, and entered into their rest. And here was the church of the New Testament, in the person of the three apostles, representing all those, to the end of time, who, by faith and patience, were yet to enter in the church of the fathers and the church of the latter days—the church militant and the church triumphant—all built upon the foundation of apostles and prophets, Jesus Christ himself being the chief Corner Stone. Truly Immanuel was here in his glory, for he was here in the midst of his church, the great central object, with whom the immortals converse, and on whom the mortals gaze with awe and love. Well might Peter exclaim, not knowing, indeed, what to say adequate to such a scene, "Lord, it is good for us to be here; if thou wilt, let us here make three tabernacles, one for thee, and one for Moses, and one for Elias."

But, mark the voice which comes from heaven, as the interpreter of this scene, "This is my beloved Son in whom I am well pleased; hear ye him." There is no more need of earthly tabernacles for Moses and Elias. The times of the law, and the times of the prophets are passed. There is now a greater Lawgiver and a greater Prophet in the church below. Henceforth the only earthly tabernacle is that in which Christ resides. The work of Moses is done; the work of Elijah and all the prophets is done; but one work remains, that of the Son. "This is my beloved Son in whom I am well pleased; hear ye him." Let him be your Lawgiver, your Prophet, Priest, and King.

This whole scene of transfiguration is, therefore, a representation of Immanuel's glory in his mediatorial character, as well as the type and prelude of his estate of exaltation when he should rise from the dead, ascend to heaven, and come again in the clouds of judgment. For, most clearly, we have here the manifestation of his character as our great High Priest, properly the first of his mediatorial offices. The burden of discourse between him and the celestial visitors is his work of sacrifice. They spake of the decease which he must accomplish at Jerusalem; and the apostles are charged to tell the vision to no man till that work was done. The work of sacrifice once ended, and the great High Priest having risen again and gone up from the valley of humiliation to appear before the throne in his exalted state, a Priest for ever after the order of Melchisedec—then might this glory be declared to men.

Just as clearly is it a representation of his Prophetic character. For the apostles, and, through them, the church, to the end of time, are commanded to hear him as the great Teacher, the only true prophet and lawgiver on earth. Greater than Moses, greater than Elijah, he comes as the very Prophet of whom Moses had spoken, and whose way Elijah had already prepared in the person of John the Baptist. This vision reveals him in all the glory of the prophetic character because the prophet and the lawgiver here meet in one who is the beloved Son of God.

And so also it is a representation of the Mediator in the glory of his royal character. It was to show beforehand to a few chosen witnesses who, in due time, should bear witness to all the church how he would appear in glory when he should come as a King, a Conqueror, and a Judge. He had declared in the hearing of the multitude, only six days before, that the Son of man would come in the glory of his Father with his angels, to reward every man according to his works. And he added, that some were present, who should not taste of death, till they should see the Son of man coming in his kingdom. And here on the mountain, was the declaration verified to the three disciples who beheld this manifestation of his power and glory as the King of kings and the Lord of lords.

Altogether it forms one of the most instructive scenes in the earthly life of Immanuel. And it is full of consolation to all his people. It shows how near heaven is to us, even while in this mortal state. We are like the other disciples, left below, and wholly unconscious of what was transpiring in the mount. These heavenly visitors came and went, but they knew it not. But if our eyes were open, what glorified forms might we not behold in that spiritual world which is just above us! How thin too is the veil which intercepts our vision! It needs but death to lift it, and we shall see face to face these glorified ones. If Moses and Elias may come back into our world, and be made visible to mortal eyes, how much easier must be our transition into their world! And unto God all things are possible. Perhaps we have but to die, to realize how closely we had lived on the confines of heaven, and how true was the conception, that—

> "Millions of spiritual beings walk the earth,
> Unseen, both when we wake and when we sleep."

The beloved disciple, when writing the fourth Gospel, and quoting from Isaiah to show why the Jews rejected Jesus as their Messiah, says, "These things said Esaias, when he saw his glory and spake of him." The glory revealed to the inspired prophet was that in which he saw the Lord, sitting upon a throne high and lifted up, his train filling the temple, and the six-winged seraphim crying, one to another, "Holy, holy, holy, is the Lord of hosts; the whole earth is full of his glory." This prophetic apocalypse may be regarded as the type and prelude of the sublime vision of the transfiguration; even as the transfiguration is of that eternal kingdom and glory in which the Son of man shall be revealed at the last day. And so we find the transfiguration, with its kindred manifestations of Immanuel's glory, holding very much the same relation to the evangelical history and to all the subsequent revelations of the New Testament, which Isaiah's sublime vision held in the prophetic history and in the following Old Testament Scriptures. No doubt the apostles, in many a dark hour of toil and tribulation, remembered what they had seen and heard in the holy mount; and felt their hearts inspired with new zeal, as they looked forward to the day when their own bodies should be fashioned like unto his glorious body, and they should see him face to face. "Beloved, now are we the sons of God, and it doth not yet appear what we shall be; but we know that when he shall appear we shall be like him; for we shall see him as he is. And every man that hath this hope in him, purifieth himself, even as he is pure."

CHAPTER VIII.

HIS SUFFERINGS AND DEATH.

THE death of Jesus was itself a sublime demonstration of his immaculate virtue. So far as man's agency was involved, he died simply because a wicked world could not longer bear the presence of such virtue. His pure and holy life was a standing rebuke to its iniquity. He had committed no crime, he had done no wrong, he had spoken no treason; his whole public and private life had been a mission of mercy, goodness, and peace; and he boldly challenged the world, in whose open daylight all his deeds had been done, to convict him of a single sin; and the world, in a most remarkable manner, admitted that he was unimpeachable of any crime. The witnesses who appeared against him contradicted each other. The man who betrayed him acknowledged his innocence, and hung himself in remorse for his own crime. The judge who passed sentence of death upon him, confessed in the same breath that he could find no fault in him. The Roman executioner testified at the cross that he was a righteous man. The powers in authority at Jerusalem knew that for envy alone he had been betrayed and delivered up; and all the people from Dan to Beersheba knew, that his miracles had been miracles of mercy; his words, only words of truth and wisdom; and all his acts, acts of peace and love. And yet the world crucified him—crucified him just because it could no longer stand the reproving presence of his immaculate purity.

That such a man should have died such a death of cruelty and shame, in a civilized and enlightened age, can admit of no other explanation, when we leave out of view all the higher and Divine purposes, than that man was depraved, and he was holy. He had spoken to the guilty conscience of a world lying in wickedness as never man spake before. His heart-searching discourses had penetrated the inmost depths of its iniquity. He had proclaimed the wrath of God against all unrighteousness, and had exposed the hollow-hearted hypocrisy of the proud in the clear light of heaven's truth. With such convincing demonstration did he speak to the heart and conscience of his guilty countrymen, that they could give his doctrines no answer except that which, as they thought, should silence his voice for ever. The New Testament is full of examples of this heart-searching power of his preaching. The whole world is, to this day, full of witnesses, both among the good and the bad, of the same thing. His words do still cleave their way to the inmost convictions of every living and dying man, as no other words ever did, or can. Many others since his day have, like him, reasoned of righteousness, temperance, and a judgment to come, so as to make the wicked tremble on the very throne of power. But these have done it in his name, and in virtue of his authority and example.

It was for his fidelity, therefore, to truth and righteousness, that is, for his doctrines and his virtues, that the world put him to death. "The world cannot hate you," said he; "but me it hateth because I testify of it, that the works thereof are evil." And this unceasing testimony he had given both by his words and his virtues. His holy doctrines reproved its thousand falsehoods; and his holy life condemned its deep and dark depravity. As Socrates, at Athens, centuries before, had suffered death without a crime, save that his doctrines and his virtues rendered him obnoxious to his fellow citizens; so our blessed Lord at Jerusalem, by a similar mode of treatment, but on an infinitely higher field of truth and virtue, was rejected, betrayed, and crucified by those who could lay no sin to his charge.

But this would be to look at the death of Jesus from the human side alone; and to account for it on the low ground of a depraved human agency. Many noble martyrs have died for their opinions and their virtues in this degenerate world. It has been no uncommon thing thus to die; at least since his death. This, however, would give us no satisfactory reason for his death, looking at it from the side of his Divinity. This alone could never account for the occurrence of such a death as a part of the great unfolding scheme of Providence, and of the world's redemption. There is an infinitely higher solution. There was an infinitely grander agency at work. Wicked men committed the awful deed; but God permitted and ordained the great event, for the accomplishment of his eternal purposes of mercy to our ruined race. The Apostle Peter gave the great reason on the day of Pentecost: "Him being delivered, by the determinate counsel and foreknowledge of God, ye have taken, and by wicked hands have crucified and slain." It was no mere martyr's death he died—no patriot's immolation for his country's good—no grand moral spectacle to the universe, of virtue suffering wrongfully for virtue's sake. Whatever there was of this nature in it was the least part of it. This was merely incidental to it, and not the chief end and object of it. But it was as a sacrifice for sin—not his own but the sins of others—that Jesus died. It was as the incarnate Son of God, man's Surety, and the Mediator between God and man, that he died. He died a vicarious death. He died to satisfy the claims of God's broken law in behalf of all who believe in him, and thus to secure a righteousness for them on the ground of which they may be justified and saved. He died an atoning death, to make reconciliation for the sins of his people. For the iniquity of his people was he stricken; for the redemption of sinners through the blood of his cross, was he cut off; "He hath borne our griefs and carried our sorrows; with his stripes we are healed, and the Lord hath laid on him the iniquity of us all." Thus was it written by the prophets, and thus did it behove Christ to suffer. The Scriptures do not more clearly set before us the great fact of his death, than they do the great end and purpose of that death. "He hath made him who knew no sin, to be sin for us, that we might be made the righteousness of God in him."

He came into the world, therefore, not simply to suffer and die with us, but to suffer and die for us—to suffer and die for us as no other man ever did, or ever can. It was not simply by his example, to show us how to suffer and die; to encourage us in suffering and dying; and to sustain us in such sacrifices. Any other martyr could have done this. A thousand others have done it. We are, at all times, compassed about by a great cloud of such witnesses. But he came to do infinitely more for us than this—infinitely more than all the martyrs and confessors of all generations could ever do. He came to suffer and die for our sins, in the sense of paying the awful penalty due to them, bearing the curse of the law, atoning for our guilt, and securing our pardon and justification. He came into the world then for the purpose of suffering and dying. Thus it became necessary, or behoved him to suffer. Unlike all other human lives and deaths

—his death was not the mere natural end and consequence of living, but it was the grand, foreseen and determinate purpose for which he lived. His life was but preparatory to his death, as his death was to his resurrection and eternal glory. He became incarnate, and lived a life of self-denial and suffering, in order that he might die the death of a vicarious sacrifice for sin. In a word, the great work which he came into the world to accomplish, was a work of suffering and death, and there was no way in which it could be finished, except by passing through them.

Hence we find the Scriptures everywhere referring our salvation to the death of Christ, the blood of Christ, the cross of Christ. It is not that his labours, in working out our salvation, were restricted to the cross and to the hour of death. His whole life of spotless obedience to the law of God, formed a necessary part of his atoning work. For it became him to magnify the law and make it honourable, as well as to suffer its penalty in the room of those who had broken and dishonoured it. But it is because the shedding of his blood by the death of the cross was the great consummation of all his acts, all his sufferings. The labours and the sufferings that had gone before, found their climax and completion when with his dying breath he said, It is finished. So that from that moment, the cross became the very symbol and formula of all that Jesus did and suffered in the flesh as our Mediator. The great idea of the work of Christ is that of suffering. Hence the apostle says to the Hebrews, "It became him for whom are all things and by whom are all things, in bringing many sons unto glory, to make the captain of their salvation perfect through sufferings." Hence he said to his disciples, when these sufferings were over, "Thus it was necessary, and thus it behoved Christ to suffer." So Paul could say to the Corinthians, "I determined not to know anything among you save Jesus Christ and him crucified;" and to the Galatians, "God forbid that I should glory save in the cross of our Lord Jesus Christ." Indeed the sufferings of Christ, which had been for ages the theme of prophecy, from David to Isaiah, and from Isaiah to Zechariah, become in the New Testament the prominent and inexhaustible subject of all his apostles. The preaching of the gospel is the preaching of the cross. For the joy set before him, he endured the cross, despising the shame; and it is through the blood of the cross that he hath made peace between God and man, and reconciled all things unto himself, whether they be things in earth or things in heaven.

It is true that our Saviour's life had something of joy as well as suffering. No holy heart, however oppressed and burdened with others' woes, can be utterly without joy. It can glory even in tribulations; it can rejoice in conscious innocence and in a sense of God's favour amid its very tears. So in his suffering and sorrowful life there were some gleams of bright, celestial joy, notwithstanding the dark eclipse which necessarily excluded his Divine nature from mortal view. There were times when Jesus rejoiced in Spirit and said, "I thank thee, O Father, Lord of heaven and earth, because thou hast hid these things from the wise and prudent, and hast revealed them unto babes: even so, Father, for so it seemed good in thy sight."

Still the predominant feature, both of his life and of his death, that is, of the whole period of his humiliation from the manger to the cross, was suffering, self-denial, sacrifice. It is not possible for any human mind to know, or even to conjecture, all that a holy being, constituted as he was and dying the death he died, must have endured in the way of suffering. Nevertheless, with the sacred narrative before us, we may get some idea of it, by considering carefully some of the many elements which made up that bitter cup. And to do this we must take into account those which preceded as well as those which attended his dying hours.

The first element of his sufferings was the deep poverty and privation of his life. This began in the manger of Bethlehem, and it followed him to the tomb. "Ye know the grace of the Lord Jesus Christ," says an apostle, "that whereas he was rich, yet for our sakes he became poor." Being originally "in the form of God, and counting it no robbery to be equal with God, he made himself of no reputation, and took upon him the form of a servant, and was found in the likeness of men." He emptied himself of all his titles, all his honours, all his riches, and became a man of poverty, who had not where to lay his head while living, and in death was buried in the tomb of his friend. Though Lord of all, and rightful possessor of the riches of the universe, he yet on earth toiled for his daily bread till his public ministry began, and during that ministry was supplied from day to day in a manner that could not be unattended with hardship and want. Whatever degree of mental or of physical suffering may be conceived of as attending this voluntary surrender of all the bliss of heaven, and all the comforts of earth, for a life of extreme dependence and of pinching penury, may well be regarded as forming at least one of the ingredients of that bitter cup, which our blessed Lord had to drink. With what sadness, with what tenderness, and yet with what uncomplaining submission does he say, "The foxes have holes and the birds of the air have nests, but the Son of man hath not where to lay his head!"

The next element was the humiliation and shame that in the eyes of an ungodly world attended such a life and such a death. "Being found in fashion as a man, he humbled himself and became obedient unto death, even the death of the cross." He was despised and rejected by men; he was despised and we esteemed him not. "The reproaches of them that reproached thee fell on me." In all his career he had to encounter the opposition, the derision, the insults of a wicked world. And he had to bear it alone. There was none to cheer him, none to succour, none to defend his injured character. Consider him, says an apostle, who endured such contradiction of sinners against himself. He stood and proclaimed the truth of God in the midst of a crooked and perverse generation, and at every step of his pathway he was watched by malignant foes, who were plotting his destruction, and doing every thing in their power to blacken and blast his character. For three years he bore this cross, despising the shame. And when at last his hour was come, he died amid scenes of mockery and insult, in which all that Jew and Gentile, earth and hell could do, was done to pour contempt upon his suffering soul. Forsaken by his friends, scourged, mocked, crowned with thorns by the officers of justice, laughed to scorn, taunted, and spit upon by his relentless persecutors, and dragged away faint and bleeding to the place of execution ; he is nailed by merciless and ruffian hands to the accursed cross of a Roman slave, and hung up between two thieves, with every possible circumstance of disgrace and torture that human ingenuity could invent to heap infamy upon its dying victim.

Another element of his suffering life was its ceaseless toil. From the opening of his public ministry till its close in death he never rested. His whole life was spent in the two great departments of his labour—healing the maladies of the body, and the deeper maladies of the soul. His disciples, at times, besought him to rest and to take food. But his answer was: My meat is to do the will of him that sent me, and to finish his work. I must work while the day lasts; the night cometh when no man can work. I have a baptism to be baptized with, and how am I straitened till it be accomplished? The zeal of thine house hath consumed me. Hence we find him everywhere thronged by the vast multitudes that had come to be healed, and to hear his preaching. He went about doing good, preaching in all the cities and villages, instructing all who came to him, attending upon all the great festivals at Jerusalem; and the probability is strong, that during the few years of his public ministry, all his cotemporaries both in Judea and Galilee, as well as strangers from all parts of the world, had heard his matchless instructions and seen his mighty works. Never was there on earth a more active, self-devoted, and laborious life. His days were consumed in toil, and whole nights in prayer to God

> "Cold mountains and the midnight air
> Witnessed the fervour of his prayer,
> The deserts his temptations knew,
> His conflicts and his victory too."

Another bitter ingredient in his cup of suffering, was that mysterious agony which oppressed him in immediate view of the cross. In the garden of

Gethsemane, on the night of his betrayal, before a single pang of death had come, there was an awful crushing weight of woe upon his holy soul, which seemed to fill him with an unearthly and unutterable sorrow, and caused his bodily frame to sweat drops of blood. This mental anguish, the fit exponent of that load of imputed guilt which he was bearing for a lost world, and which revealed its power so fully in the garden, was not indeed limited to that dark hour. It had, doubtless, been his daily and nightly companion long before, and during all his ministry. Omniscient as he was, and foreseeing the end from the beginning, with all the vivid distinctness that we perceive present or past events, the whole scene of death was ever present to his thoughts; and it is impossible that he should not often, especially when alone, have suffered the same agony that oppressed him in the garden. For during all his life, as well as on the cross, he bore our griefs and carried our sorrows, because the Lord had laid on him the iniquity of us all. On the mount of transfiguration he had talked with Moses and Elias of that decease which he should accomplish at Jerusalem; and we have the record of many different occasions on which he had plainly told his disciples, that he must go up to Jerusalem, to be betrayed by the rulers, delivered to the Gentiles, and crucified. All this long anticipated and new sorrow of the soul, in immediate foresight of death, and under the infliction of Divine wrath against the sinner's substitute, comes upon him in the garden and at the deepest gloom of midnight. And he has to bear it alone, unsupported and uncheered, save as he is strengthened for the trial by the ministering angels of God. The world, for which he is about to die, is asleep; his disciples, the companions of his three years' toils, are all heavy with sleep. Jerusalem, the city of his love, is profoundly asleep, all save those murderous bands that are moving at this lone hour towards his place of sorrow. And there he is in the garden's deepest shade, in the midst of his sleeping disciples, prostrate on the ground, sweating, as it were, great drops of blood falling down to the ground, now breaking the silence with the cry, "My soul is exceeding sorrowful even unto death," and now with the thrice offered prayer to the Father, "If it be possible let this cup pass from me; nevertheless not my will but thine be be done." Here was sorrow, here was suffering such as mortal heart had never felt—such as no finite mind can fully fathom.

"It was a dark and fearful hour,
The stars might well grow dim,
When this mortality had power
So to o'ershadow him;
That he who gave man's breath might know
The very depths of human woe."

The next element to be noticed in our Saviour's sufferings was the physical torture of his crucifixion. Outside of the dungeons of a Roman Catholic Inquisition, there has probably never been devised by man, a mode of death more dreadful and excruciating than that of the cross. Indeed the intensest torture both of body and mind, we are accustomed to describe by this very term, *excruciating*, which is derived from the cross. But in our Saviour's case, besides all the common and inevitable horrors of such a death—its ignominy, its laceration of the flesh, its exhaustion, its thirst, its lingering agony—there was added every thing in the way of insult, derision, and cruel torture which a diabolical rage could invent to augment his sufferings. To such an extent was this carried, that the insane malignity of his foes defeated itself, and brought on a premature and unexpected sinking of his vital powers. So that the scene of torture, which in ordinary cases, was protracted through several days, was terminated in his case by death in a few hours. In the fresh vigour of health and in the strength of manhood, he is arrested at dead of night, brought to trial with the early dawn, hurried before the bar of the Sanhedrim, then before Pilate's bar, then before Herod and his men of war, and then back to Pilate, and then again through the streets of the city to the hill of death, bearing his cross; and through all these scenes he is so maltreated, by being scourged with rods, smitten on the head, pierced with a crown of thorns, reviled and spit upon, that when at last exhausted with fatigue, and faint with loss of blood, he is nailed to the cross, his poor crushed nature yields to the load of agony, and he expires in from three to six hours. The probability is that it was the shorter period, for while the evangelists vary as to the beginning of this dread drama, some speaking of the sixth hour, and some of the third, they agree that there was darkness over all the land from the sixth to the ninth hour; so that we have reason to think, our blessed Lord was nailed to the cross about the sixth hour or mid-day, and expired about the ninth hour, near the time of the evening sacrifice, and thus suffered during the three awful hours of this supernatural darkness. But in either event he suffered all that human malignity could inflict in the way of torture, and all that was required to extinguish such a life. There is no page in human history, no record of human sufferings, which recounts a scene more calculated to touch the heart by its graphic grouping of all that was dreadful in the persecutor, with all that was sacred and tender in the sufferer, than this story of the passion of our Lord.

But another still, and probably the bitterest of all the ingredients in our Saviour's cup of suffering, was the hiding of his Father's face in that dread hour of agony. While his faint and bleeding body was suffering all that it could suffer at the hands of man, his pure and holy soul was suffering still more under the awful hidings of his Father's face. It was something of this kind, no doubt, realized or anticipated, that, on the night before, had so overpowered him, when he sweat great drops of blood, and said, "My soul is exceeding sorrowful, even unto death." But now, in his extremity, when dissolving nature hangs helpless on the cross, when earth and hell have risen in league against him, when all human helpers have forsaken him and fled, save one trembling disciple and his heart-broken mother with her female attendants—now when earth's deepest darkness has gathered over his dying head, that favour, and love, and fellowship which from all eternity he had enjoyed with his Father seems to be withdrawn, and the very heavens are turned to wrath. All the waves and billows of Divine wrath seem to be passing over his head, and he is left alone to struggle with that overwhelming despair which, but for him, had been poured for ever upon the soul of sinful man. His last words had been spoken, his last charges given to his weeping mother and the loved disciple, his last promise to the penitent thief had been uttered, his last petition had been offered up for his foes: "Father, forgive them, they know not what they do;" the raging, scoffing multitude around had exhausted all their vials of wrath upon him, and now, it seemed that nothing remained but to die. But at this awful moment there is a loud and bitter cry, as of one sinking in despair. "And, at the ninth hour," says the evangelist, "Jesus cried with a loud voice, saying, Eloi, Eloi, lama, sabacthani! which is, being interpreted, My God, my God, why hast thou forsaken me?'

And here we may well veil our faces in astonishment, and hush our lips to silence. No mortal tongue may tell of the nature or the extent of that suffering which thus in death weighed down the Spirit of the Son of God. The Scriptures have left it in impenetrable mystery. The human mind is incapable of comprehending it. All that we know, or perhaps could know in our present state, is that he suffered not thus for himself. To his pure and holy soul, death itself could have had no terrors. To him death would have been but the gate of endless joy; and instead of this cry of despair, there would have been but songs of triumph. It was because he was bearing in his body on the cross the sins of the whole world, dying the Just for the unjust, and receiving into his bosom the awful curse of the violated law, which, for the time, shut out from his view every ray of the Divine favour—it was because he stood in our place and died our death, that there was for a season poured out upon his devoted and vicarious head the unmitigated wrath of God against sin. This was the burden of his fearful passion. "Thus it was written, and thus it behoved Christ to suffer, and to enter into his rest." But this storm of wrath was soon passed. And then he said, "It is finished." And when he had cried again with a loud voice, "Father, into thy hands I commend my spirit," he bowed his head and gave up the ghost.

CHAPTER IX.

HIS RESURRECTION AND ASCENSION.

THE story of the cross, whilst it is the most tragical, is yet the most glorious in the annals of history. The sufferer becomes a conqueror, even in his death; because he dies to rise again triumphant and victorious over all his foes. Where the historic record of all other men ends, that of Jesus begins with a new and nobler life. With him the pangs of death and the three days of imprisonment in the sepulchre were but the door of entrance for his glorified humanity, into that sublime and exalted estate in which there is no suffering and no death for ever.

It is impossible for us to appreciate fully the feelings of his disciples as they passed through the sad scenes of his crucifixion. We can never, even in imagination, stand under that crushing grief and despair which pressed them down, when hope after hope departed, and they, at last, beheld the beloved Master, on whom all their fondest affections centred, expire on the cross. Because we know what they did not. We know the end from the beginning. We see the cross and the crown together. We read the sad story of suffering and woe in the light and the joy of his resurrection morning. The rising sun of the third day does for us what it could not do for them—it throws back a halo of glory which gilds the Saviour's tomb, and dispels for us all those doubts and fears which had gathered over their souls, as the gloom of midnight. Still, with the glorious issue full in view, there is a deathless pathos to all hearts, in the story of the cross. Though we know that the third day morning shall be as life from the dead, shall dry up our tears and tell of our great deliverer's almighty power, and pour again the sweet radiance of hope into the broken hearts of his scattered disciples, still there is a touching tenderness in the sufferings of Jesus, which the millions yet to come, as the millions who have gone before, can read of only with tearful eyes.

No doubt, some of his disciples cherished a hope, even to the last, that his life would be spared; that in some way he would exert his mighty power, even on the cross, to the confusion and overthrow of all his enemies. Judas himself, probably, had some idea of this sort when he betrayed him; and this may have been one reason why the traitor was so overwhelmed when he saw that instead of being delivered by his miraculous powers, he was actually sentenced and led out to death. Though the guilty traitor had, in despair, hung himself, we cannot suppose that his faithful and loving disciples could have lost all hope of deliverance, so long as life lingered in the sufferer. Scattered and dismayed as they all were by the rude midnight arrest of their Master, some of them, nevertheless, had gathered sufficient courage and hope to follow him through all the scenes of the trial, and to the very place of execution. Wherever they may have stood among the crowd, near by or distant from the cross, in silence and fear, watching every shifting scene of the dreadful tragedy, it could not be otherwise than that they should have prayed, and expected, even to the last moment, that he would come down from the cross. Because they had for three years seen too many manifestations of his Divine power, not to know that with him nothing was impossible. He saved others, even after death had done its work; and why might he not save himself from the approach of death?

But when they saw him die, apparently before the usual time of death by crucifixion; when, after three hours of supernatural darkness veiling the hill of death, and three hours of unparalleled sufferings, they heard his last words, "Father, into thy hands I commend my spirit," and saw him bow his head and give up the ghost—as they gazed in helpless agony upon the pale, still form of their beloved Lord, every ray of hope must have departed from their stricken hearts, and they were left in utter desolation. They thought it had been he who should have redeemed Israel. But they could think so no longer now!

As the sun of that awful day went down thus in darkness and blood, all their hopes of earthly, and, perhaps, of celestial glory, went down with it. What a night was that in Jerusalem! What a night to Peter and John! to Lazarus and his sisters! to Mary Magdalene and his own heart-broken mother! As they met one another that night or the next Sabbath day, and ventured to recount the scenes of trial and death they had witnessed, to tell of his last words, his last looks, and his dying agony, how their hearts must have sunk at the sorrowful recital! The Scripture is silent as to all that they did, said, and suffered during this period. All that we know about their feelings we learn from the record of Luke, that "many beholding the things that were done, smote their breasts and returned;" and from the words of Jesus to two of them after he was risen, "What manner of communications are these that ye have, one to another, as ye walk, and are sad?" But that they cherished his memory with an intense and undying affection, we may safely infer, not only from the honourable burial he received at the hands of Joseph and Nicodemus, and the costly preparations of the women for embalming his body, but from all the incidents connected with the amazing scenes of the resurrection, the forty days' sojourn with them, and his glorious ascension to heaven.

Though our Saviour had repeatedly foretold the

manner of his death, and declared plainly to his disciples that he would rise again the third day, still the scenes of his trial and crucifixion were so extraordinary and overwhelming, that they seem to have obliterated all thought or expectation of this kind, as effectually as if he had never spoken a syllable on the subject. While his enemies remembered these predictions, and resorted to all possible safeguards against being imposed upon by his friends, there is no indication that in all Jerusalem he had a single disciple or friend who once thought of his rising again. The loving women, who, if any on earth, would have clung to such a hope, instead of thinking of a resurrection, went at the appointed hour to the grave to embalm his dead body. And so far was such a thought from their minds, that the most ardent of them all, Mary Magdalene, even when she saw the stone rolled away from the sepulchre, the grave clothes lying alone, and two angels sitting on the spot where the body had lain, still inquired of him, whom she supposed the gardener, where he had borne away the dead body. Indeed, as if to account for that strange forgetfulness of his predictions, and slowness of heart to believe, which had taken possession of their minds, the sacred writers tell us expressly that his disciples did not understand the Scripture that he should rise again.

Under these circumstances, how convincing must have been the proof which overcame this reluctance to believe, and how overpowering the joy, when, on the third day, the strange tidings got wing, and flew from heart to heart, that Jesus was alive again. Never, perhaps, in the history of mankind, was there a day of such joy to so many desolate hearts, as that first day of the week in Jerusalem. The accounts given by the evangelists of the whole scene —so fragmentary, so full of rapid movements, so full even of apparent disorder and confusion, different messengers running in different directions with the news, some meeting and some missing each other—are in perfect keeping with all that is natural on an occasion so marvellous, and so fraught with unspeakable joy. There is nothing in all the New Testament truer to life and nature, and more convincing by all its internal evidences, than the manner in which this story of the resurrection of our Lord is told by the different evangelists. If such an event had to occur a thousand times over, in precisely the same, or similar, circumstances, it could not occur without producing just such phenomena as we find it did produce among the saddened, despairing, and yet loving friends of Jesus—first the slowness of heart to believe, then the fright and bewildered astonishment, then the eager haste to spread the tidings before the whole truth was known, then the unutterable joy which the great fact inspired, and then some appearance of discrepancy in the different statements made by the different parties, as they recounted the several different parts of the scene.

It is worthy of remark that there was no human spectator of our Lord's resurrection. His disciples expected no such event, and were not looking for it. It occurred at an hour when Jerusalem was all quiet in the slumbers of the early morn. The keepers on guard, who were awake, were terrified at the apparition of angels, and became as dead men. And when the women reached the spot, it was only to hear the announcement, "He is not here; he is risen as he said; come see the place where the Lord lay." But the stupendous scene was past. While men slept, and ere the earthquake had rent the rocks and broken the profound stillness of his three days' sojourn in the tomb, the conqueror had burst asunder all its bars and risen to life again. Thousands had gazed upon him in the deep humiliation of the cross. They had witnessed all his agonies; had heard his outcry; had seen him die; had followed him to the burial. But no mortal eye looked on him, as in might and majesty he rose! In this he was seen of angels alone. They were his witnesses. They bore testimony of the fact to his unbelieving disciples one after another; and they, in turn, bore testimony to an unbelieving world. And thus the most wonderful and stupendous event in the history of man—the event on which all our hopes of heaven depend, was at the first received on testimony, the testimony of angels witnessing it, and the testimony of his disciples reporting to others what they had heard and seen.

But the proof was not to end with this testimony. Although no human being saw him rise from the dead, yet many were permitted to see him, to converse with him, to eat with him, after he had risen. To see one die and laid in the grave, and then to see him alive again, is as perfect an evidence of his resurrection as to behold him in the very act of rising. And this evidence the apostles had repeatedly, in a great variety of circumstances during a period of forty days. In this sense we find on different occasions from one to five hundred eye-witnesses of his resurrection. Luke tells us, that to his chosen apostles he showed himself alive after his passion by many infallible proofs, being seen of them forty days, and speaking of the things pertaining to the kingdom of God. We have an account of at least ten different occasions on which he appeared to some one or more of his disciples, during this period. He may have appeared to them on many other occasions of which we have no record. We know he appeared often enough to convince the most sceptical and unbelieving among them.

His first appearance was to Mary Magdalene alone, early in the morning, immediately after the other women had gone back to the city to tell the disciples of the vision of angels which they had seen at the sepulchre. It is a pleasing and instructive fact that this devoted female disciple, whose chief distinction was her ardent love, should thus be honoured with the first interview with the risen Redeemer. The interview was short, but full of tender pathos. She stood weeping in the garden, grieving for the loss of the absent body, for it was not in the tomb, and she knew not where they had laid it. The living Saviour had already said, "Woman, why weepest thou? whom seekest thou?" But in the intensity of her grief she knew him not. He had, however, but to speak her name, Mary, probably in that very tone to which she was accustomed while he was alive, and then she turned and said with the full joyous gush of recognition, "Rabboni!" which is to say, Master! Jesus saith unto her, doubtless for the purpose of turning her mind from all mere earthly affections, and making her feel that he was no longer an inhabitant of this world, "Touch me not; for I am not yet ascended to my Father; but go to my brethren and say unto them, I ascend unto my Father and your Father, and to my God and your God."

His second appearance was immediately after this to the other women, Joanna, Salome, Mary the mother of James and others, as they were on their way to the city, when he met them, and said, "All hail." And they came and held him by the feet and worshipped him. In this embrace of his feet there was, no doubt, the homage of believing, reverential, and adoring worship; and hence he receives and does not forbid it, as he had just done in the case of Mary Magdalene, whose first gushing emotions of joy had centered upon him more as an earthly friend restored, than as a glorified God and Saviour. Then said Jesus unto them, "Be not afraid; (they were still awed by his spiritual majesty,) go tell my brethren that they go into Galilee, and there shall they see me."

His third appearance was to Simon Peter, some time during this first day of the week; for in the evening of that day, we find, as the two disciples returned from Emmaus, that they were greeted at Jerusalem with the tidings, "The Lord is risen, indeed, and hath appeared unto Simon." As the Apostle Paul in mentioning his different appearances to the Corinthians, says, "He was seen of Cephas, then of the twelve," we naturally infer, that on this occasion he appeared to Peter alone, and before he had appeared to any of the twelve. We have no record, however, of any of the incidents of this third appearance. The reason why Peter was singled out from all the other apostles, and permitted to see his risen Master first, could hardly have been because he had always been a sort of leader among his brethren, but is, no doubt, to be found in the great grace and condescension of our Saviour, who would thus display his loving kindness by visiting and reassuring the very disciple who had offended most grievously, and was now most deeply humble and penitent. If the Lord had indeed forgiven and appeared to Peter, how much more might all the others take courage and be comforted!

His fourth appearance was on the same day to two of those who had believed in him as the Redeemer of Israel, as they journeyed to Emmaus and talked together of all that had happened. The whole story of this interview, which is given by Luke with peculiar minuteness of detail, is full of interest, as showing the deep grief and disappointment which his sorrowful death had brought upon all his friends. Joining himself to them as a stranger, with interest and sympathy listening to all their sad recital of what had just occurred at Jerusalem, then himself expounding to them the Messianic Scriptures in a way that made their hearts burn within them, and at last reaching the village, and yielding to their solicitation to tarry with them for the night, he reveals himself to them at their evening meal, in the act of breaking, blessing, and distributing the bread. No doubt, in those significant and familiar acts, there was something on this occasion, in his whole tone and manner, which brought all the past vividly to their minds, and made them see, as though scales had fallen from their eyes, the living face of Jesus. With astonishment and joy they rose up that hour, and went back to Jerusalem to tell the great truth which the women had reported in the morning, and which till then they had doubted, that the Lord had risen indeed. When they reached the city, they found the eleven and other disciples gathered together. And then there was a mutual announcement of glad tidings. For while the two travellers rehearsed what things were done on the way, and how he was revealed to them in the breaking of bread, the Jerusalem company even anticipated their story with the exultant statement, "The Lord is risen indeed and hath appeared unto Simon."

Then follows quickly his fifth appearance to this assembled company, even as they talked and rejoiced together. "And as they thus spake, Jesus himself stood in the midst of them, and saith unto them, Peace be unto you. But they were terrified and affrighted, and supposed that they had seen a spirit. And he said unto them, Why are ye troubled? and why do thoughts arise in your hearts? Behold my hands and my feet, that it is I myself; handle me and see; for a spirit hath not flesh and bones as ye see me have. And when he had thus spoken, he showed them his hands and his feet. And while they yet believed not for joy, and wondered, he said unto them, Have ye here any meat? And they gave him a piece of a broiled fish and of an honeycomb. And he took it and did eat before them [thus giving the most palpable proof that he was a living man]. And he said unto them, These are the words which I spake unto you, while I was yet with you, that all things must be fulfilled, which were written in the law of Moses, and in the prophets, and in the psalms concerning me. Then opened he their understanding that they might understand the Scriptures. And he said unto them, Thus it is written, and thus it behoved Christ to suffer, and to rise from the dead the third day; and that repentance and remission of sins should be preached in his name among all nations beginning at Jerusalem. And ye are witnesses of these things. And behold I send the promise of my Father upon you; but tarry ye in the city of Jerusalem until ye be endued with power from on high."

These five appearances were all on the first day of the week, the first Christian Sabbath. His sixth appearance was on the Sabbath following, or eight days after, to the eleven disciples including Thomas. Thomas had not been present at the former interview. When the others reported to him how they had seen the Lord, had conversed with him, eaten with him, marked the very nail prints on his hands and feet, in a spirit of excessive caution and incredulity he replied, "Except I shall see in his hands the print of the nails and put my finger into the print of the nails, and thrust my hand into his side, I will not believe." Our blessed Lord, more perhaps with a view to make the proof of his resurrection doubly sure to the doubtful of all coming generations, than of yielding to the unreasonable demand of this doubting disciple, granted another interview, probably in the same room, which removed all the doubts of Thomas. "Then came Jesus, the doors being shut, and stood in the midst and said, Peace be unto you. Then saith he to Thomas, Reach hither thy finger, and behold my hands; and reach hither thy hand and thrust it into my side, and be not faithless but believing. And Thomas answered and said unto him, My Lord and my God. Jesus saith unto him, Thomas, because thou hast seen me, thou hast believed; blessed are they that have not seen, and yet have believed."

His seventh appearance was on the shore of the sea of Galilee, early in the morning, to seven of his disciples, who had spent a toilsome and fruitless night in fishing. John, who narrates it, calls it the third time he had showed himself to his disciples. It was indeed only the third time he had appeared to any collective body of them, but as we have seen, the seventh, from the first, including the four preceding interviews, which were only personal, as being with one or two individuals. The disciples on this occasion were Peter, James, John, Thomas, Nathaniel or Bartholomew, and two others, whose names are not given. This interview, which is perhaps more fully recorded than any other, was accompanied by one of his mighty miracles, bringing to their minds other similar displays of Divine power while he was with them, and leading them at once to know that it was the Lord. On this occasion he dined with them, and held that memorable dialogue with Peter, which seemed intended to reinstate him in his forfeited apostleship, and to point out the great duty of the office—"Feed my sheep, feed my lambs."

His eighth appearance was that which he had himself appointed in Galilee. On the night he was betrayed, he had said to his disciples, "When I am risen I will go before you into Galilee." On the morning of the resurrection the angels sent word to his disciples by the women, and he afterwards met them and repeated the message, To go and tell his brethren to meet him in Galilee. Accordingly after the second Sabbath his apostles seem to have left Jerusalem and returned to Galilee to wait for his appointed appearance. We know not the place which he appointed. The Scripture speaks of it as a mountain, and tradition makes it the mount of transfiguration, on which Peter, James, and John had once beheld his excellent glory, when he charged them to tell the vision to no man till the Son of man should be risen from the dead. It seems very natural to suppose that there was some sort of connection between that first partial revelation of his glory to the three disciples, and this fuller manifestation to all of them after he was risen from the dead, and that the place was the same. But be this as it may, there can be no doubt that a great number of his disciples and friends, not only from Jerusalem, but from all the cities of Galilee had resorted to the place of meeting. It is evidently of this interview that the apostle Paul speaks, when writing to the Corinthians many years afterwards, he says, "After that he was seen of above five hundred brethren at once, of whom the greater part remain unto this present, but some are fallen asleep." Important however as the occasion was, both in its previous appointment, and in the numbers who witnessed it, it is very briefly recorded. "Then the eleven disciples went away into Galilee into a mountain where Jesus had appointed them. And when they saw him they worshipped him, but some doubted. And Jesus came and spake unto them, saying, All power is given to me in heaven and earth." Matthew, who alone of the evangelists, relates this appearance in Galilee, connects with it the words of the great commission, "Go ye therefore and teach all nations, baptizing them in the name of the Father and of the Son and of the Holy Ghost, teaching them to observe all things whatsoever I have commanded you, and lo, I am with you alway, even unto the end of the world." And the strong probability is that this great command was given on more than one occasion—at least on this one, and on that in which he ascended to heaven.

The ninth appearance was to James, as mentioned by Paul in his first epistle to the Corinthians. There is some doubt as to which one of the persons bearing the name of James, this was. In all probability it was the one whom Paul mentions in his epistle to the Galatians as the "brother of the Lord," and who was afterwards eminent in the church at Jerusalem, and took a leading part in the first synod there, as stated in the fifteenth chapter of the Acts. But there is no account given elsewhere of this appearance to James.

His tenth and last appearance (excepting that in which he was afterwards seen by Paul) was on the day of his ascension to heaven. A full account of this is given by St. Luke, partly in his Gospel and partly in the first chapter of the book of Acts. It occurred forty days after his resurrection, and consequently just ten days before the day of Pentecost. No doubt the whole band of his apostles, having returned from Galilee, were present at the last interview. Indeed we read in immediate connection, that the number of the names of those who were together was one hundred and twenty. On this occasion he charged them not to depart from Jerusalem, but to "wait for the promise of the Father, which they had heard of him. For John truly baptized with water but ye shall be baptized with the Holy Ghost, not many days hence." From Luke's narrative we should infer that he spent some considerable time with them on this occasion, "giving them commandments and speaking to them of the things pertaining to the kingdom of God." As suggested by Dr. Moore, in his admirable little work, "The Last Days of Jesus," we think it likely that he met his disciples on this occasion, as he had done on others, in the evening, in their usual place of meeting in Jerusalem, spent the whole night with them, and led them out through the early dawn, by the familiar path which they had trodden on the night of his betrayal, across the brook Cedron, past Gethsemane, and over the Mount of Olives, to his loved and quiet Bethany, the chosen spot for his ascension. Luke closes his Gospel with the following record: "And he led them out as far as Bethany, and he lifted up his hands and blessed them. And it came to pass while he blessed them, he was parted from them, and carried up into heaven. And they worshipped him, and returned to Jerusalem with great joy, and were continually in the temple praising and blessing God. Amen." In the Acts, he supplements this account with other interesting particulars. The disciples ask, "Lord, wilt thou at this time restore again the kingdom to Israel?" He answers, "It is not for you to know the times or the seasons, which the Father hath put in his own power. But ye shall receive power, after that the Holy Ghost is come upon you; and ye shall be witnesses unto me both in Jerusalem, and in Judea, and in Samaria, and unto the uttermost part of the earth." In all probability he uttered again the solemn words of the great commission, "Go ye into all the world, and preach the gospel to every creature; he that believeth and is baptized shall be saved; but he that believeth not shall be damned. And when he had spoken these things, while they beheld, he was taken up; and a cloud received him out of their sight." St. Mark adds, "He was received up into heaven and sat on the right hand of God." "And while they looked steadfastly toward heaven, (continues St. Luke,) as he went up, behold two men stood by them in white apparel; who also said, Ye men of Galilee, why stand ye gazing up into heaven? This same Jesus who is taken from you into heaven, shall so come in like manner, as ye have seen him go into heaven. Then returned they unto Jerusalem, from the Mount called Olivet, which is from Jerusalem a Sabbath day's journey."

Truly the Lord hath done all things well! Nothing could be more complete and convincing than these proofs of his resurrection, given to so many witnesses, in so many varying forms, through the space of forty days. Angels saw him rise. But men saw him die, saw him buried, saw him alive again, and saw him ascend to heaven. There can be no possibility of mistake as to either of these facts. There is no more ground to doubt that he rose from the dead and ascended to heaven than to doubt that he lived and died. But if he rose and ascended, then all is true, all is sure and safe for ever. If he rose and ascended, then is he a Divine and Almighty Saviour, exalted at God's right hand and living for evermore to intercede for us. If he rose and ascended, then was his life an incarnation of God in the flesh, and his death a great atoning sacrifice for the sins of the lost. If he rose and ascended, then is this story of the cross a true gospel to a perishing world, the power of God and the wisdom of God to all who believe. If he rose and ascended, then is our hope of heaven secure, our salvation on the immovable basis of God's truth and God's infinite love and mercy. Then was he delivered for our offences, and raised again for our justification. Made of the seed of David according to the flesh, he was thus declared to be the Son of God with power by the resurrection from the dead.

Nothing ever was, and nothing ever can be, more sublime and glorious than such a termination of such a life, and such a death! The toils of his suffering life, the humiliation and agony of his cruel death, exchanged for the immortal robes of his resurrection body, and for the bright diadem of a conqueror over death and hell, ascending to his eternal throne in the heavens. The genius of the old classic Greeks and Romans, strove to embody some lofty conception of the sublime and beautiful, the eternal and divine, in their myths and fables of human apotheosis and transformation. But here, alone, in Jesus Immanuel, incarnate, crucified, risen, ascended, and crowned with glory, we find the only true meeting of earth and heaven, the one grand transformation of the Divine into the human, and apotheosis of the human on the throne of Divinity. Here alone, in this wondrous and sublime story, do we find man's only possible exaltation and glory. We see not yet all things put under man; for the end is not yet. But we see Jesus on the throne; we see Jesus, "who was made a little lower than the angels for the suffering of death, crowned with glory and houour; that he, by the grace of God, should taste death for every man."

The resurrection and ascension were not only a demonstration to the universe that his grand work of atonement for man by the death of his cross, was fully accomplished and accepted in the heavens, but a complete and eternal vindication of his character and all his claims as our conquering King and Redeemer. It marked the ending of his estate of humiliation in the flesh as our atoning sacrifice, and the beginning of that estate of exaltation and glory, as King of kings and Lord of lords, in which he shall reign in heaven and rule on earth, until all enemies shall be put under his feet, and death itself shall die. It was a fitting spectacle to the attendant angels, that the whole band of loving disciples, as on that memorable morning they stood on the mount, and saw him ascend in his chariot of cloud to the highest heavens, should, with adoring wonder, worship such a Saviour, such a conqueror. It was but the prelude of that eternal worship which awaited him on high, when the everlasting doors were lifted up at his approach, and the decree of welcome went forth—"Let all the angels of God worship him."

CHAPTER X.

HIS MEDIATORIAL OFFICES AND WORK.

AMONG men no character can be fully estimated without considering the offices filled and the works accomplished by its possessor. It is mainly through the works of a life time that the character of any man is best displayed. The same rule will apply to the life and character of our blessed Lord. Thus far we have traced the great facts and events of his life, with his Divine and human virtues, through their gradual historical development, from the hour of his incarnation in human form to that of his ascension to heaven, as our risen and glorified Mediator. And if this were all, it would infinitely transcend anything that was ever known among men; but the wondrous story does not end even with this sublime apotheosis. As he came from heaven at first only to enter upon his work, as he passed from life to death only to finish for ever one great part of that work, that of sacrifice and expiation, so he passed from death to life again, and from earth to heaven itself, but to carry on and consummate his great Mediatorial work. Having done all that the case he had undertaken required to be done on earth, he is now gone up to appear before God as our Advocate, Intercessor, and victorious King, there to accomplish all that part of his work which, from his ascension to his second coming, remained to be done.

Although exalted on his heavenly throne, he still fills his Mediatorial offices, and is carrying on his great work, and we, in this mortal state, only see in part and know in part what he has done and is yet to do; nevertheless the Scriptures have revealed enough to give us some conception of his character and achievements as our Prophet, Priest, and King. These three great offices pertain to him as Mediator between God and man; and they belong to him both in his estate of humiliation and of exaltation. For whilst the different offices are, each in turn, most prominently brought to view at the several successive stages of his work, those of Prophet and Priest characterizing his estate of humiliation, the one in his life of instruction, and the other in his death of sacrifice, and that of King characterizing his state of exaltation from the resurrection to the consummation of all things; still all three of them were filled by him while in the flesh, and by anticipation for four thousand years before the advent, and all three of them are still borne by him, now that he is in heaven. As our Great High Priest, he finished the work of sacrifice, by the one offering of himself upon the cross. But he is still our Great High Priest in heaven—"a priest for ever after the order of Melchisedec"—"a priest who ever liveth to make intercession for us"—"the Lamb slain from the foundation of the world." In the days of his earthly ministry he was the Prophet, that was to come into the world, the great Teacher of Israel, a light to lighten the Gentiles, and a preacher of glad tidings to the poor. But from the very beginning, through all dispensations, he was in the church as the great Prophet of all the prophets, teaching his people and preparing the way for his incarnation, by revelations and manifestations to holy men of old who spake as they were moved by the Holy Ghost. In his kingly office, which belongs preëminently to his estate of exaltation and glory, as risen from the dead and ascended to heaven, he is now seated at God's right hand, clothed with all power in heaven and earth, conquering all his and our enemies, and carrying forward his eternal purposes, until "every knee shall bow, of things in heaven and things on earth and things under the earth, and every tongue shall confess that he is Lord of all to the glory of God the Father." But still he was our King from the beginning of the history of Redemption. In the darkest hour of his humiliation, when his Godhead was all eclipsed in the cloud of mortal flesh, and he stood arraigned as a culprit at Pilate's bar, he could say, "I am a king, for this end was I born, and for this purpose came I into the world, that I might bear witness unto the truth." He was with his church through all the wilderness, not only as her suffering Messiah, but as her all-conquering Sovereign—the Prophet of all her prophets, the Priest of all her priests, the King of all her kings, the rightful Lord of the whole earth. And thus, from the beginning to the end, through all dispensations, both in humiliation and in exaltation, in life, in death, and resurrection, on earth and in heaven, he executes for the church of his redeemed his great Mediatorial work, and fills all the high offices of Prophet, Priest, and King. His kingdom is an everlasting kingdom, and of his dominion there shall be no end, till he shall have consummated all the purposes of his Mediatorship, shall have put down all authority and power, brought all his ransomed home to glory, and delivered up the kingdom to God the Father, that God may be all in all.

If we look back into the history of the ancient church, as developed through all the Old Testament Scriptures, it is in the light of these three great Mediatorial offices filled by the Messiah, that we can best understand the types, symbols, ceremonies, and revelations of that time of preparation. All spoke of Christ, all pointed to Christ as the one Mediator and Deliverer of Israel—the Prophet to come, like unto Moses, the atoning Priest adumbrated by Aaron, the eternal King in Zion sitting on the throne of David. He was the burden of all the prophets' messages of salvation and deliverance. He was the subject of all the inspired bards and psalmists of

Israel. He was the substance of all the burning altars, the bleeding victims and the priestly offerings and oblations. He was the end of all the laws for righteousness to every one that believeth. He was the theme of all the Scriptures, that were written in the law, the prophets, and the psalms. It is only as the soul of man is taught and enlightened by him, as God's appointed Prophet, redeemed from sin and hell by him as God's accepted Priest, delivered from all enemies by him, as God's equal and eternal Son, the King of kings and Lord of lords, that any soul ever was or can be saved. It is only thus as he executes those great offices, and in them accomplishes the greatest work that was ever undertaken in the universe, that all the church of God, of all nations and generations from the beginning to the end of time, shall be saved and gathered home to glory, washed by his blood, sanctified by his Spirit, and redeemed by the might of his power.

There was in the very nature of the work which the Mediator undertook, the work of redemption, a necessity that he should discharge each of these great offices. The race of man was ruined by sin, apostate from God, under the curse of his violated law, lost to all the light of heaven, and delivered over to the dominion of death. To make reconciliation for such sinners—lost for ever in the triple sense of being in utter darkness, in utter condemnation, and utter bondage to death and the devil, there was a threefold work to be done, the work of instruction, the work of sacrifice, and the work of conquering all their enemies. The pall of nature's darkness must be lifted from eyes that had been hopelessly blinded by sin. The death penalties of a violated law must be met and satisfied for those who were already under its curse, having forfeited every claim to life. The prison-doors of hell and the grave must be unbarred by one, who, having infinite righteousness, and having given his own blood as a ransom, had almighty power to release the captives. Thus it was written, and thus it behoved Christ to suffer; and not only to suffer, but to pour the light of Divine truth into every sin-blinded soul, and to reign and conquer in behalf of all his redeemed people. It is therefore of the very essence of salvation, a matter arising out of the fearful exigencies of our condition as sinners, that our Mediator Immanuel should be a Prophet, a Priest, and a King. The whole history of redemption exhibits him as such. He could not have been a Saviour otherwise. In each his work is perfect and glorious. He taught with infinite wisdom, as never man taught. He died once for all, the victim and the priest, the just for the unjust, as neither men nor angels could have died. He destroyed Satan's throne, and triumphed openly over death and hell, as none but a God could do. Not in one jot or tittle of all his work did he fail.

If we look forward into the Apocalypse, the prophetic book of the New Testament, we behold him, amid all the glories of the heavenly hierarchy, worshipped and adored; not only for his own infinite majesty as the eternal Son of God, but for that amazing work of redemption which he had wrought out by his blood, carried forward by his Spirit, and perfected for ever by his sovereign power as the Mediator between God and man. This is indeed the sublimest vision of the Apocalypse. This work of the Lamb is the theme of the new song. It is the most wondrous, the most joyous, and exultant theme that the angels had ever heard in heaven. "And they sung a new song, saying, Thou art worthy to take the book and to open the seals thereof; for thou wast slain, and hast redeemed us to God by thy blood out of every kindred and tongue and people and nation; and hast made us unto our God kings and priests; and we shall reign on the earth. And I beheld, and I heard the voice of many angels round about the throne and the living creatures and the elders; and the number of them was ten thousand times ten thousand, and thousands of thousands, saying with a loud voice, Worthy is the Lamb that was slain to receive power, and riches, and wisdom, and strength, and honour, and glory, and blessing. And every creature which is in the heaven, and on the earth, and under the earth, and such as are in the sea, and all that are in them, heard I saying, Blessing and honour and glory and power be unto him that sitteth upon the throne, and unto the Lamb for ever and ever."

It is in this work of man's redemption that Immanuel has made the highest manifestation to the Universe of the glory of God. Not only does it display the infinite loveliness of his own personal character, as showing the riches of his grace toward perishing man, and the glory of his power and wisdom in his salvation, but it displays, as nothing else had ever done or could do, all the grand, essential attributes of the Godhead. "These things the angels desire to look into;" for these, more than all works and ways of God, declare his glorious moral character, as the God of infinite justice, infinite holiness, infinite truth, infinite love and mercy.

By this great work of sacrifice, of instruction, and of conquest, he has vanquished all the enemies of God for ever, has rolled back the night of sin and death from the face of God's creation, broken Satan's power in the dust, reconquered and reclaimed his trophies, and prepared a people for his glory in the heavens. On this work he has founded his own Mediatorial kingdom, and built his church, so that the gates of hell shall not prevail against it. This church of the redeemed, founded on the rock of ages, in his own person, gathered from every age and nation, and intended by him to make known unto principalities and powers in heavenly places, the manifold wisdom of God—this church is itself but the result and exponent of his mighty work. And not until the last sinner shall have been saved, and the last saint of all earth's teeming millions brought home to glory—not until the general assembly and church of the first born, who are written in heaven, shall have met to part no more in his presence—not until that day when God shall wipe all tears from every face, and these mortal bodies, raised from the dust and fashioned like unto his glorious body, shall have rejoined their ransomed spirits in the skies, shall we ever know all that God our Saviour has done for us.

"Burst, ye emerald gates, and bring
To my raptured vision,
All the ecstatic joys that spring
Round the bright elysian.
Hark, the thrilling symphonies
Seem e'en now to seize us,
Join we too the holy lays,
Jesus, Jesus, Jesus.
Sweetest sound in Seraph's song,
Sweetest note on mortal tongue,
Sweetest carol ever sung,
Jesus, Jesus, Jesus"

CHAPTER XI.

HIS SECOND AND GLORIOUS APPEARING.

It is a blessed and glorious thought that the Son of God is to come back to the earth again—not in poverty and humiliation, but in triumph and majesty—not as the Lamb slain, but as the Lion of the tribe of Judah. "I know that my Redeemer liveth," cried the sorrowing patriarch of Uz, "and that he shall stand at the latter day upon the earth. And though after my skin worms destroy this body, yet in my flesh shall I see God; whom I shall see for myself, and mine eyes shall behold, and not another, though my reins be consumed within me." The law of compensation reigns through all the ways of God. The cross is but the prelude to the crown. The death of a good man is but his stepping stone to glory. And so the first advent of the Son of God in weakness, and toil, and woe, was but the necessary preparation for that second advent in which he is to come in all the glory of his Father with the holy angels. He shall stand upon Mount Zion again, not as he once stood, derided and rejected of men, at Pilate's judgment-seat, but himself the Judge of quick and dead. "This same

Jesus," said the angels at his ascension, "who is taken up from you into heaven, shall so come in like manner as ye have seen him go away into heaven." "Behold he cometh with clouds," writes the prophet of the Apocalypse, "and every eye shall see him, and they also that pierced him shall see him, and all kindreds of the earth shall wail because of him." One of the earliest prophecies on record, speaks of this second and triumphant coming. Enoch, the seventh from Adam, said, "Behold, the Lord cometh with ten thousands of his saints, to execute judgment upon all, and to convince all that are ungodly among them of all their ungodly deeds which they have ungodly committed, and of all their hard speeches which ungodly sinners have spoken against him."

This sublime doctrine of the second coming our Saviour had often taught his disciples while he was with them: "When the Son of man shall come in his glory and all the holy angels with him, then shall he sit upon the throne of his glory; and before him shall be gathered all nations; and he shall separate them one from another, as a shepherd divideth his sheep from the goats." When arraigned for trial before the Jewish Sanhedrim, and adjured by the high priest, in the name of the living God, to tell them whether he was the Christ, the Son of God, he answered, "I am; and hereafter shall ye see the Son of man sitting on the right hand of power, and coming in the clouds of heaven." And thus from the time of his ascension to heaven, onward through all the Epistles and the Apocalypse, we find this grand doctrine of his return to earth, held forth prominently, as the great prophecy of the New Testament, and the most joyful hope of the church. "We look for that blessed hope," says Paul, "the glorious appearing of the great God, even our Saviour Jesus Christ."

To the Scriptures of the New Testament, and to the whole church of the New Dispensation, this promise of the second advent, stands related, very much as the promise of the first advent stood related to the Scriptures and the church of the Old Covenant. It is the grand inspiring object of hope. It is the bright pledge of final deliverance and redemption for all the saints of God.

Intimately associated with this second coming of the Son of God, are many of the grandest revelations of the Scriptures—the resurrection of the dead, the judgment of men and angels, the new heavens and the new earth, the final redemption of the church, the glory of the righteous, the doom of the wicked. All these last great things are dependent upon his advent. They belong to him in his exaltation and glory. They are to be executed by him in his royal power. To all the universe, they will be as full a display of his Divine power, and as triumphant a vindication of his right to reign and rule, God over all, blessed for ever, as the death of the cross had been of the completeness of his work of humiliation and sacrifice. Here we behold one of those amazing contrasts of which the history of redemption is so full—the Son of God condemned as a man at Pilate's bar, the Son of man vindicated as God on his throne of judgment in the clouds. If ever, in any case, the end and issue of a story justified its beginning and vindicated all the stages of its progress, so as to furnish by the very fitness and symmetry of all things a demonstration of its truth, it is done in the history of Redemption. Man in his impotent short-sightedness, looking only at the feeble beginnings, and the partial progress of this scheme of salvation across the ages, may be tempted to write imperfection and failure upon the Gospel of God. But let man suspend his judgment till the whole case is issued—till the last great things are done—till the Man of sorrows and the scenes of Gethsemane give place to the judgment-seat of Christ, and the "glory yet to be revealed" —till heaven shall compensate for the toils of earth and eternity adjust the inequalities of time—and he shall then see, that from the beginning to the end, in every step of his progress, the Lord hath done all things well.

As the crucifixion fulfilled the prophecies of four thousand years; as the resurrection and ascension demonstrated the Divine purpose and significance of the crucifixion; as the descent of the Spirit on the day of Pentecost was but the development of the great results of the resurrection and ascension;

as the onward, irresistible progress of the gospel among the nations for eighteen centuries, is but the carrying out of that Pentecostal beginning, and the constantly accumulating vindication of all that has gone before; so the shout of the archangel, the trump of God, and the coming of the Son of man in the clouds of heaven, attended by the spirits of just men made perfect, and all the holy angels, to raise the dead, to judge the world in righteousness, and to settle all the issues of time in the light of eternity, will be but the necessary unfolding and completing of that great scheme of Providence and grace which began with the first announcement in Eden—"The seed of the woman shall bruise the serpent's head." The whole progress of the work with its crowning day, was as fully present to the mind of the Lord then, to justify and direct every successive revelation of the Bible, as it will be before the minds of angels and men at the last day.

As to the time appointed for the ushering in of these last great things, the Scriptures have given us no distinct information. We may perhaps understand something, as to the order of succession in which they are to occur, and get some faint conception as to their awful grandeur, transcending all earthly and mortal scenes; but the set time is one of those secret things, which belong not to us or our children, but only to God. It is a great mystery, over which the Divine mind seems purposely to have thrown the veil of concealment. Many have sought in vain to penetrate that veil; to see what is behind the curtain of the future. From the very days of the apostles there have been some in the church, who have striven to fix the time of Christ's appearing. St. Paul wrote his second letter to the Thessalonians, in part to correct the error of those who taught that the coming of the Lord was then just at hand. At many subsequent periods, down to our own, the same opinion has been revived; and some have ventured beforehand to tell the year and the day when the Son of man should appear. Some even now, from their reading of the prophecies, are looking with confident assurance to his appearing as an event near at hand, to be witnessed by this generation. Some suppose that his coming will not be until the earth has had its full week of working days—a thousand years for a day—to be followed by a seventh day of rest, or Millennial Sabbath, of a thousand years; making four thousand years of preparation for the first advent, two thousand for the second, and one thousand of the latter day glory for the end.

But all such conjectures are fruitless, perhaps presumptuous. When on the mount of Olives, the disciples came to our Saviour privately, saying, "Tell us when shall these things be; and what shall be the sign of thy coming, and of the end of the world?" after telling them of many things which must first come to pass in all nations, he added, "But of that day and hour knoweth no man, no, not the angels of heaven, but my Father only." And when, on the day of his ascension to heaven, they asked, "Lord, wilt thou at this time restore the kingdom to Israel?" he said, "It is not for you to know the times and the seasons which the Father hath put in his own power." It would seem, that such language as this, even though referring to other events, ought to deter us from any confident assertion as to the time of his second and glorious appearing; and also as to the question whether his coming shall long precede, or be immediately followed by, the stupendous scenes of the resurrection of the dead, the last judgment, and the destruction of the world by fire. About scenes so awfully sublime as these, and so unlike any thing that mortal eye has gazed upon, and of which the sacred writers speak with such reserve, it is certainly rash for us to speak with confidence, either as to the time or programme of their occurrence. The revelations of the Apocalypse on this whole subject, are as yet a profound mystery, it may be, reserved for the clearer light of ages yet to come, and providences yet to be unfolded. The best thing we can do on such a subject, is to lay aside all speculation, and ponder well the simple, but sublime words of the apostles. "If we believe, that Jesus died and rose again," says Paul to the Thessalonians, "even so them also that sleep in Jesus will God bring with him. For this we say unto you by the word of the Lord, that we who are alive and remain unto the coming of the Lord, shall not prevent (rise before) them who are asleep. For the Lord himself shall descend from heaven with a shout, with the voice of the archangel and with the trump of God; and the dead in Christ shall rise first. Then we who are alive and remain shall be caught up together with them in the clouds, to meet the Lord in the air; and so shall we ever be with the Lord." With this accords what he says to the Corinthians, "Behold, I show you a mystery. We shall not all sleep, but we shall all be changed, in a moment, in the twinkling of an eye, at the last trump; for the trumpet shall sound, and the dead shall be raised incorruptible, and we shall be changed. For this corruptible must put on incorruption, and this mortal must put on immortality. So when this corruptible shall have put on incorruption, and this mortal shall have put on immortality, then shall be brought to pass the saying, that is written, Death is swallowed up in victory. O death, where is thy sting? O grave, where is thy victory? The sting of death is sin, and the strength of sin is the law; but thanks be to God, who giveth us the victory through our Lord Jesus Christ." With this also agrees the solemn language of St. Peter, "The day of the Lord will come as a thief in the night; in the which the heavens shall pass away with a great noise, and the elements shall melt with fervent heat, the earth also, and the works that are therein shall be burned up. Seeing then that all these things shall be dissolved, what manner of persons ought ye to be in all holy conversation and godliness, looking for and hasting unto the coming of the day of God, wherein the heavens being on fire shall be dissolved, and the elements shall melt with fervent heat. Nevertheless, we, according to his promise, look for new heavens and a new earth, wherein dwelleth righteousness."

It ought to be enough for us to know that he shall come again in glorious majesty; that it is one of the sure promises of God; that it is among those unchangeable decrees, every jot and tittle of which shall stand fast, though heaven and earth pass away. It ought to be enough for us, that it is not only revealed as certain, but like the coming of death, as imminent to all generations of men. As no man or angel can say when it shall come; so none can say when it shall not. It is certain; it will be sudden, even as the lightning of heaven; and it may be soon. The closing message of the Apocalypse is, "He which testifieth these things, saith, Surely, I come quickly. Amen. Even so, come, Lord Jesus." Like the first advent, this second coming is to live, as a fresh perennial hope, in the heart of the church until it is realized in glorious fruition. It is to bring unmingled joy and glory to all God's children, not only at the close, but through all the stages of the pilgrimage. From the first it was intended to pour a stream of holy joy, by anticipation, along the whole track of ages, as generation after generation of the saints has loved and longed for his appearing. All the grand events in the history of redemption have been so arranged as to throw their celestial radiance both forward and backward over the course of time. It was so with the first advent. It has been and will be so with the second. The saints who live before, and those who come after, are partakers of the same blessed influences with those who are cotemporary with the transactions. Faith resting on the testimony of inspired history in God's word looks back to the cross of Calvary, as for four thousand years it looked back to the first promise in Eden. Faith and hope, resting in like manner on the sure voice of inspired prophecy in God's word, looks forward now to this glorious revelation of the Son of God from heaven, even as, for four thousand years, they pointed the eye of every believer to the first manifestation of the Son of God in the flesh. And thus with faith looking back to rest on all that God has said and done, with hope looking forward to rest on all that he is yet to do, and love looking up to rest on all that he is in his own glorious person and character, the whole economy of salvation is so arranged, that, in whatever dispensation of the church the believer's lot is cast, he has all the fulness of the blessings of the gospel of Christ, for Christ is ever with him, and Christ is all in all.

CHAPTER XII.

THE SAVING POWER OF HIS GOSPEL.

ALL these great facts and doctrines connected with the person, character, offices, and work of Christ taken together constitute the gospel. The essence of the Bible is the gospel; and the essence of the gospel is Christ. In the history of Christ, in his life, character, labours, sufferings, death, resurrection, ascension, and Mediatorial reign, we find the great truths of Divine mercy and grace, which every sinner must embrace in order to be saved, and which God has revealed as the glad tidings of great joy to all people. "This is a faithful saying, and worthy of all acceptation, that Christ Jesus came into the world to save sinners."

This story of Immanuel reveals the way and the only possible way of salvation for any soul of man. It contains the only facts, the only remedy, the only influences, which meet all the fearful exigences of our lost condition. To believe this story in all its fulness is to inherit everlasting life. To reject it is to perish utterly and for ever.

The Apostle Paul gives a striking summary of the great facts of this gospel, in their immediate connection with Christ, when he says, "Without controversy, great is the mystery of godliness, God was manifest in the flesh, justified in the Spirit, seen of angels, preached unto the Gentiles, believed on in the world, received up into glory." These, indeed, are the essential facts of the gospel, without which it would be no gospel. It is only because Christ, the Son of God, is in it, as the power of God and the wisdom of God unto salvation, that it has any efficacy in saving a soul from death, and in reclaiming a world from sin. As Christ therefore is the sum and substance of the gospel, and we have undertaken to unfold his glorious life and character as exhibited in all that he hath done and suffered; having thus far spoken of him in his varied estates, labours, gifts, virtues, instructions, offices, miracles, and mighty works, as Immanuel, the Mediator between God and man, it remains only to complete our view by a brief survey of that gospel which is the great result or effect of his work. This gospel is the church's great treasure; the world's richest inheritance; and this, with all its blessed influences, its priceless hopes for time and eternity, we owe to Jesus. In the course of ages there have been many great benefactors of mankind, who have toiled, suffered, and died, to leave posterity a legacy of good. There is but one benefactor who has left mankind a gospel of Divine grace and salvation. Let us mark well the secret of its power. "The weapons of our warfare," says the apostle, "are not carnal, but mighty through God to the pulling down of strong holds."

First of all the gospel carries with it the convincing and enlightening power of the truth. It is a system of truth—the very truth which God reveals. Resting all its claims upon the evidence of facts, and appealing for the reality of its facts to the testimony of God and man, it challenges the scrutiny, the conviction, the belief, the homage of every rational mind. It addresses the understanding and the conscience of every human being. It speaks to his reason, to his instincts, to his deepest experience. In the name of God it demands a hearing; and then on the broad basis of infallible proof, it demonstrates itself to be worthy of all acceptation. And thus, as the accredited truth of God, it claims the assent of that whole intellectual and moral nature which God has given to man for the very purpose of knowing and obeying the truth. The human soul was made for truth, eternal truth. It must feed on truth; it must grow by truth, as the very law of its being, the aliment of its subsistence. Nor can it reject the truth without doing violence to its nature. In like manner, as the soul is God's workmanship, created with capacities to know and follow the truth, the gospel is God's workmanship—a perfect system of Divine truth—revealed and offered to man in his darkness and impotence for the purpose of restoring to him that light of truth and that life of God in the soul, which he had lost by sin.

By his gospel, therefore, as a system of Divine, eternal truth, revealed for man's salvation, Christ speaks to all the world, as never man spake. The Bible is full of examples, and the world itself, wherever this gospel has been preached, is full of examples of that moral power by which his words find a response in the deepest convictions of our nature, and cleave their way to the inmost experience of every living man. When he reasons of righteousness, temperance, and a judgment to come, as he did in the days of his earthly ministry, and as he does through all the sacred pages by his prophets and apostles, men feel that their very consciences are made manifest, and that they are open and naked to the eyes of Him with whom they have to do. Conscious guilt trembles, like Felix, on the very throne of power. He slays them by the breath of his mouth. His word of truth is quick and powerful, sharper than any two-edged sword, piercing even to the dividing asunder of soul and spirit, of the joints and marrow, and is a discerner of the thoughts and intents of the heart. In this convincing and enlightening power over the human mind, and in this mastery of conscience, there never has been anything on earth like the gospel.

But it is remarkable, that, while revealing to us the only way of salvation from sin, Christ has taught the world its most important lessons on a thousand other subjects. This gospel has been found to be the great reformer and civilizer of man. We behold in it not alone the power of God and the wisdom of God unto salvation to every one that believeth, but the true moral life of all nations. It contains all the truth of God respecting the road to heaven and the hope of immortality. It also contains the most important truth yet known to man, respecting all the highest and best interests of the present world. It is the true elevator of all human society. It is the only civilizer and peacemaker among the nations. There is a far-reaching wisdom in this gospel, which, from the beginning, has seemed to comprehend the whole problem of man's wretchedness, to provide for all his wants, to anticipate all his boasted discoveries in art and science, and to make him feel, even to the end of the world, that in its presence, he is but a child and a learner.

The highest attainment which moral philosophy has yet made only carries us back to the words of Jesus as its most fitting formula, "Whatsoever ye would that men should do to you, do ye even so to them, for this is the law and the prophets." Our whole theory of civil and religious liberty, as founded upon a total separation of church and state, seems to have been comprehended in that memorable saying, "Render therefore to Cæsar the things that are Cæsar's, and to God the things that are God's." The wealth of nations, the progress of society, the peace and prosperity of the world, the true political economy for all mankind, were all announced in the maxim, "Put up thy sword, for they that take the sword shall also perish by the sword." After eighteen centuries of toil, of study, and of advancement, it is remarkable that the last analysis of all our mental, moral, political, and social science, only carries us back to the simple and sublime, yet incidental, utterances of this gospel, for its truest and best exponent.

Again; this gospel vindicates itself as the power and wisdom of God, because it comes to man with all the attractive and constraining power of Divine love. It reveals God as the God of love; it exhibits God in Christ, reconciling the world unto himself by the cross; its great plea with man is, that "God so loved the world that he gave his only begotten Son, that whosoever believeth in him should not perish, but have everlasting life;" and its universal proclamation is, "Ho, every one that thirsteth, come ye to the waters. And the Spirit and the Bride say, Come, and let him that heareth say, Come, and let him that is athirst come, and whosoever will, let him take the water of life freely." It is a gospel of love, conceived in the infinite love of God the Father, executed in the amazing self-sacrificing love of God the Son, and applied by the constraining love of God the Spirit. Flowing from the inexhaustible fountain of Divine love, all other love excelling, its effect is love—universal love of man to his brother man, and eternal love of man to his redeeming God. We love him because he first loved us. Love is the moral philosophy of the gospel. Love is its grand motive, by which faith works, purifying the heart and overcoming the world. Love is the fulfilling of all its laws. Love is the vital principle of all its obedience. It is by the power of love that it wins the human heart, and gains all its proudest triumphs over the world, and the flesh, and the devil. There is, perhaps, nothing which more distinguishes the gospel from all the systems and devices of human philosophy, and demonstrates it to be the mighty power of God, than this wonderful manner in which it has revealed the love of God. It has thus bound the human heart in chains of everlasting love to God, and encircled the earth with a network of holy influences, which shall one day bring it in willing and adoring homage to Immanuel's feet.

Still further, this gospel makes its appeal to the heart of every living and dying man, as nothing else has ever done or can do, because it carries with it the power of a Divine consolation. It is the friend and helper of the wretched, the perishing, the lost. It is the only thing on earth that can speak peace to the troubled soul, and whisper hope in the ear of the dying sinner. When all other resources fail, when friends and comforters have all forsaken us, when the very cords of life are breaking, and nothing is left us but to die, there is a voice here which can give us courage and consolation amid the darkness of the valley and shadow of death. Through all the trials of life, and all the dangers of dissolving nature, the soul that hath laid hold upon the hope of this gospel, can look up, with calm confidence, and say: "Thou art with me, I will fear no evil. Thy rod and thy staff, they comfort me." Here is the patience of the saints. Here is the hope of the blessed. Here is the strong consolation of the cross. He, who was touched with the feeling of our infirmities, who hath borne our griefs and carried our sorrows, who was bruised for our iniquities, and had the chastisement of our peace laid upon him, who passed through the iron gates of death before us, and was made perfect through sufferings, hath spoken to us, by his gospel, such words of consolation as never man spake. Clothed in all the tender compassions of our mortal nature, and, at the same time, arrayed in all the glorious attributes of the Godhead, having authority on earth to forgive sins, and power to destroy all the enemies of our souls, he was able to offer strong consolation to all the sons and daughters of sorrow. While upon earth he spake, and now that he is gone up to glory he still speaks, in all the invitations and offers of this gospel, words of pardon, of peace, of comfort, of loving sympathy, of grace and mercy, such as mortal tongues have never spoken, such as human ears had never heard before. "To you, O men, I call, and my voice is to the sons of men! Come unto me, all ye that labour and are heavy laden, and I will give you rest. Take my yoke upon you and learn of me, for I am meek and lowly in heart, and ye shall find rest unto your souls."

To the weeping sisters at the grave of Lazarus, he said, as he alone could say, "Thy brother shall rise again. I am the resurrection and the life. He that believeth in me, though he were dead, yet shall he live. And whosoever liveth and believeth in me shall never die." To the poor, blind Bartimeus, on the way-side as he passed by at Jericho, who rose and pressed towards him through the crowd, crying, "Jesus, thou son of David, have compassion on me," he said, "Go thy way, thy faith hath made thee whole." On the last great day of the Feast of Tabernacles, he stood and cried in the hearing of the thousands of Israel, and of the officers who had been commissioned to arrest him, with accents of love and mercy which ought to have melted the hearts of all that dying multitude, "If any man thirst, let him come unto me and drink." To his faithful but sorrowing disciples, on the night before he suffered, the last night he was to be with them on earth, he spake those precious and memorable words so full of love, so overflowing with Divine consolation: "Let not your heart be troubled; ye believe in God, believe also in me. In my Father's house are many mansions. I go to prepare a place for you. In this world ye shall have tribulation; but be of good cheer, I have overcome the world. Peace I leave with you;

my peace I give unto you; not as the world giveth, give I unto you." To the poor penitent thief on the cross at his side, who turned to him his dying eyes and prayed, "Lord, remember me when thou comest into thy kingdom," he said, "This day shalt thou be with me in Paradise."

And still that voice of love and mercy, that voice of hope for the perishing, and strong consolation for the penitent, sorrowing soul, is ringing through all the world. In the wretched abodes of poverty and sin, in the dark prison houses of sin and shame, this gospel still utters its proclamations of mercy from the Lord, saying, "Come now, and let us reason together, saith the Lord. Though your sins be as scarlet, they shall be as white as snow; though they be red like crimson, they shall be as wool." From the beginning it has been preached to the poor. It is adapted to the deepest necessities and wants of the poor. It comes and offers its richest consolations without money and without price. Wherever wretchedness can cry for mercy and helplessness can trust, there may all its saving power be felt. In the chambers of disease and suffering, where heart and flesh are failing fast, and the world is receding from the view of the dying, there its voice of consolation may be heard in strains as sweet as angels use, whispering peace to the soul. In the silent cemeteries of the dead—on all their marble monuments, over all their solemn gateways and sepulchral arches, graven with an iron pen and lead in the rock for ever, are inscribed the words of this gospel—the living words of Jesus. And there are no other words on mortal tongues which can take their places. In the sacred presence of our buried dead, in the darkened chambers of the suffering sick, and on all those occasions where human hearts lie crushed and bleeding in the dust of affliction, we instinctively feel, that there are no words fit to utter except the words of Jesus. These alone are sacred enough for our sorrow. And these alone can tell us of hope, of immortality, of Divine consolation.

But, last of all, and above all, this gospel is the mighty power of God for the pulling down of the strongholds of sin and Satan, because it is ever accompanied by the energies of the Divine Spirit, the third person of the adorable Trinity. We must not forget that, while the gospel is the special result of the work of Christ, it is at the same time the united work of all the persons of the Godhead. It is, in fact, a revelation and a manifestation of the Triune God, requiring the work and agency of each adorable person in the unfolding of its scheme of mercy, and displaying, in turn, both to men and to angels, their glorious attributes and character. In this, more than in any other work of his hands, God has unfolded the riches of his grace and glory, in making known to us the mysterious union of Father, Son, and Holy Ghost in the Godhead.

In analyzing the elements of influence over man,

as wielded by the gospel, we have seen that it carries with it, first, the mighty power of Divine truth, and then the attractive power of Divine love, and then, again, the power of Divine consolation; and that, having all these inherent elements of success, it is adapted to do the work and accomplish the end for which God designed it. But there is another power —a power over and above all these, which is absolutely essential to their efficiency. It is the power of the Spirit of God. It is that Divine power which sets all the other powers of truth, and love, and consolation to work. It is a power not lodged in the gospel like truth, and love, and consolation, which can act only as it is acted on, but ever coming down from above to accompany the gospel wherever it is preached, in order to apply its truth, to unfold its love, and give its consolation to the heart of man. This is the grand secret of all its efficiency and success in opening the eyes, winning the hearts, and saving the souls of dying men. This is the special work and office of the Holy Ghost—to apply the gospel and make it effectual to our salvation.

Still, in contemplating the gospel as the result of the work of Christ, this agency of the Holy Ghost must be included. The Comforter, according to the eternal covenant of redemption, and according to his promise when he departed, was sent forth from the Father, to take his place in the church and to carry on his work. Christ's only true Vicar and Representative on earth is this Comforter, the Holy

Ghost. Hence the whole work of the Spirit in the hearts of men is, in one sense, the work of Christ, even as in another sense it is also the work of the Father. This Divine agency of the Spirit, in applying the truth of God to the hearts of men, and so making the redeeming work of Christ effectual to their salvation, was only a part of the grand economy of grace. While each person of the Godhead fills his own office, and performs a special work, they all work together in such a manner, that what one does may be ascribed to the others also. Our Saviour was explicit on this point, when he said, "My Father worketh hitherto and I work. I came not to do mine own will, but the will of him that sent me, and to finish his work. I do nothing of myself, but as my Father hath taught me, I speak these things. And he that sent me is with me; the Father hath not left me alone; for I do always those things that please him." The same intimate union of purpose, and communion in work which thus existed between the Father and the Son, even while the Son was on earth, also exists between the Spirit and the Son, now that the Son hath ascended to his mediatorial throne, and the Spirit, in the bosom of the church below, is still carrying on his work. And so this power of the Divine Spirit, which accompanies the preached gospel, even as from the beginning of revelation it has inspired the word of God in all the Scriptures, and made that word effectual to salvation, may be regarded as one grand department of the work of Christ. The Spirit itself, like all the other blessed influences of the gospel, is the gift of Christ, and the very purchase of his death. "If I go not away, the Comforter will not come to you, but if I depart, I will send him unto you. And when he is come he will teach you all things, and bring all things to your remembrance, whatsoever I have said unto you. He shall reprove the world of sin, and of righteousness, and of judgment to come."

While, therefore, the Spirit is the Comforter sent by Christ to communicate the consolations of the gospel, he is also the great reprover to enforce upon the conscience of man, all its doctrines, precepts, promises, and warnings. And this Divine Instructer is always in the bosom of the church, to accompany and make effectual the preaching of the word: "Go ye and teach all nations: lo, I am with you always, even to the end of the world." Though this treasure of truth divine is borne by earthen vessels, yet its efficiency is of God. Man works and God works. And God hath chosen the weakness of man's agency in the work of preaching this gospel, that the mighty power might be seen to be of God. And thus it is that the gospel is sure of success—final and complete success. Despite of human weakness and folly, despite of open enemies and false friends, foes without and traitors within, over all the opposition of earth and hell, it shall triumph gloriously. God will not let it fail. "He shall see of the travail of his soul and be satisfied," is the promise to the Mediator. And this is the grand office and end of all the Spirit's work in the soul—to make the work of Christ for the soul effectual to its complete salvation.

Well might the apostle say, "I am sure, that when I come unto you, I will come in the fulness of the blessing of the gospel of Christ." He felt that this story of the cross which he preached was indeed a gospel of good things, complete in all its parts, adequate in all its powers, worthy of God and man. It is, indeed, full of incomprehensible wonders, mysterious doctrines, far above reason's grasp, amazing scenes, past and yet to come, which can be received only on the testimony of God. But it is just as full of great facts, and heart experiences, and plain palpable doctrines which every sane man knows to be true, and to be the most important of all truth. And perhaps the most amazing thing of all is, that any human being can reject it: that, in a world of darkness and death, where there is no other light, and no other possible chance of life, guilty, dying man should turn away in his impotent folly, spurning the only arm that can save him. Surely the greatest of all sins—the most unreasonable, the most unaccountable, and the most fatal, is the sin of unbelief—the sin of rejecting the Son of God. How would it strike the mind of man with astonishment, if he could see such a spectacle among the fallen angels, as that which this world now presents to the universe in the case of every unbelieving sinner! If God had visited the lost angels with such mercy, and such offers of life as he makes to us in the gospel, what would man think if he should see all hell arrayed in opposition to God's ambassador; despising every overture of reconciliation; and, at last, rising up in wrath against him, as man rose against the incarnate Son of God? What would man think if he could see the immaculate Son of God visiting the lost and ruined spirits of the pit, in their dark abodes; standing with them for a season on the burning soil of hell; paying their penalty and bearing their curse as he did ours; offering them redemption through his blood as he does to us; weeping over their sin and folly in all the tenderness of Divine compassion; saying as he did to the sinners of lost Jerusalem, "Oh thou that killest the prophets, and stonest them that are sent unto thee, how often would I have gathered thee, as a hen doth gather her brood under her wings, but ye would not!" and then, at last, as rejected, despised, crucified, he dies at their hands, crying, "Father, forgive them, they know not what they do," and all in vain because of their unbelief! But this is not the sin of devils. It is the sin of unbelieving men.

Unbelieving men, in their amazing folly and wickedness, reject this gospel, notwithstanding all its evidences, all its promises of life, all its manifestations of Divine love and mercy. They see no beauty in it that they should desire it. Though angels desire to look into it; though the world is full of the trophies of its power; though heaven is already peopled with myriads of happy spirits, redeemed through its blessed influences; though kings, and prophets, and nobles of the earth looked forward through distant ages, rejoicing in its glad tidings; and apostles could say, "God forbid that we should glory save in the cross of our Lord Jesus Christ, by whom the world is crucified unto us and we unto the world;" still unbelieving men, who have their all at stake upon the issue—a heaven to gain, or a heaven to lose by it—see no beauty in Immanuel, no glory in this gospel of God's grace. "He was in the world, and the world was made by him, and the world knew him not." Through his preached gospel, and by the mighty working of his Spirit, everywhere bearing witness in the hearts of men to the truth and power of that gospel, he is still in the world; the world has been redeemed by him; and yet the unbelieving know him not, admire him not, receive him not. In all ages past it has been true, and it is still true, that there are some to whom this glorious gospel has been hid. It is to some a savour of life unto life, to others a savour of death unto death. From the very nature of it as a remedy for sin—as God's only remedy for sin—it can leave no man as it finds him. It must cure or kill. It must save him from condemnation and give him life for evermore, or it will sink him down to a deeper and a darker woe, with the aggravated guilt of having rejected the Son of God.

The apostle John, in the opening of his history of this gospel, describes the case not only of his own countrymen, but of the men of all countries and all generations thus far, where the gospel has been preached. "He came unto his own and his own received him not. But as many as received him, to them gave he power to become the sons of God, even to them that believe on his name; who were born, not of blood, nor of the will of the flesh, nor of the will of man, but of God." The turning point in the character and destinies of men, is at the cross. All things for time and eternity hang on their reception or rejection of the Son of God. To receive him, to believe on his name, to trust in him, is to become a son of God, an heir of glory. To receive him, as he is freely offered in the gospel to every perishing sinner of our race, is to be born of God by a new, celestial birth. To reject him, to turn away from him, to find no beauty in him, is to die; because it is to reject the only remedy which God has provided for our lost estate, and to continue under that curse and condemnation which is upon us already—which is death. So that wherever the gospel goes, it must of necessity draw a line, deep, broad, and ineffaceable, between those who receive the Son of God by believing on him, and those who by unbelief reject him. Even as he declared, when, having finished the work of man's redemption, he ascended to heaven and said, "Go ye into all the world and preach the gospel to every creature. He that believeth and is baptized shall be saved; but he that believeth not shall be damned."

What then is it to believe? What is the essence of that faith in Christ by which he is received, and through which he saves the soul? "He is the power of God and the wisdom of God to all them that believe." And he commands all men every where to repent and believe the gospel. Nothing, therefore, can be more important than that we should understand what it is to believe, what it is to have a saving faith in Christ. It is the glory of the gospel that it does not leave us in any doubt or uncertainty on this essential point. It is the glory of the gospel that this one act of the soul, whereby we receive and rest upon Christ alone for salvation, whilst it is a saving grace wrought in us by God's Spirit, is as simple and intelligible as any act of man can be. It is so simple that the wayfaring man, though a fool as to other things, need not mistake it.

It is first to assent to the truth respecting Christ as true, and then to approve it as good, and then to trust the soul upon him for salvation. To see him as he is revealed in the gospel, to understand who he is, to approve and admire him as the Saviour we need, and then to renounce all other dependence, and trust in him alone for salvation—this is to receive Christ, this is to believe. It is not enough merely to assent to the truth, to understand the truth, to accept the truth as true. For ungodly men may do this as well as true believers. The truth may be held in unrighteousness. In this sense the devils believe, and yet tremble. Nor is it enough, after understanding and assenting to the truth, merely to approve and admire the truth as good. Many wicked and unbelieving men have in their inmost hearts admired the character of Christ, and given their approbation to the doctrines of the Bible. But they never came to Christ for salvation, never trusted in him. The angels in heaven approve and admire all the truth respecting the work and character of Christ. But they do not trust, they need not trust in him for salvation; and hence they cannot exercise that saving faith which is required of us. We see, then, that the essential thing in a true, saving faith, which distinguishes it from every thing else, is to trust in Christ, or commit our souls to his hands for salvation. We may understand and assent to the truth, even as wicked men and devils do; we may approve and admire the truth, even as the angels do; but any thing short of a personal trust and committing of our souls to Christ is short of saving faith.

These two things—the assent of the understanding to the truth, and the heart's approval of it as good—always accompany the act of saving faith. But alone they do not constitute it. For they may exist without it as we have just seen. We must first understand the truth before we can approve it, and we must approve it before we can trust our souls upon it. So that in every case of true saving faith there will be first an intelligent conviction of the truth on evidence, as revealed in the Scriptures, and then a moral perception and approval of it as good and necessary, and then a cordial embracing of it by trusting our souls into the Saviour's hands. "Lord, to whom shall we go? Thou hast the words of eternal life." This is the confession of one who understands the way of salvation as opened through Christ alone, whose heart and conscience approve of that way, and who has staked his own soul upon it by a personal application to Christ. Peter takes God's testimony as true, sees that he needs a Saviour, and that Christ is the only Saviour; Peter sees that this salvation through Christ alone, is not only true, but good, desirable; worthy of all acceptation as the one thing needful; and with his mind resting on this conviction of truth, and his heart filled with this moral approbation of it as good, he trusts his all to Christ for time and eternity, he comes to Christ, he receives and rests on Christ for salvation. This is faith. This is what every sinner must do in order to be saved. He must give up all other hopes, and commit his case personally to Christ. This is all that he can do. This is the very least he ought to wish to do. The act is just analogous to that of a poor sick man, labouring under some fatal malady, who has tried a thousand remedies in vain. but at last finds one physician of whose skill he is convinced, and whose mode of treatment he approves, and in the strength of these convictions, commits his case and trusts his life into his hands. So here, for all the deeper maladies of the soul there is balm in Gilead, there is a safe and skilful physician. There is but one. It is Immanuel. And the thing we have to do is to apply to him for help, to submit the case to him, to trust in him. This is the saving faith of the gospel.

Well may the apostle speak of this remedy for sin as the "glorious gospel of the blessed God." It is alike glorious in its grandeur and in its simplicity, glorious in all its Divine provisions, glorious in its adaptation to man's necessities, and glorious in the plain, equitable, and gracious terms on which it offers salvation to the perishing. It is simply, believe and live, believe what God has spoken, approve what God has done, accept what God has offered in his Son. For God has no pleasure in the death of the sinner; God, who created the soul, has given his Son to redeem it; and the great message of the gospel to every soul is, repent, believe, and live, in view of what Christ has done; for God is in Christ reconciling the world unto himself. "For God sent not his Son into the world to condemn the world, but that the world through him might be saved."

But notwithstanding the way of salvation is so plain, the terms of the gospel so easy, the character of Immanuel so attractive, and all his promises and invitations so blessed and glorious, there have always been thousands to whom all these things have been but as sounding brass or a tinkling cymbal. The human heart may be so dead to all that is bright and glorious, as not to know when its greatest good cometh. Amid the most splendid manifestations of eternal power and wisdom, there are men who can walk unconscious of the presence of a God. And so amid all the triumphs of gospel grace, and all the glories of Immanuel's person, there have been, and are human hearts that can see no beauty in him that they should desire him, and no reason why they should believe on him. He is to them as he was to the Jews of old, a stumbling block, or as he was to the Greeks, foolishness. Writing to the Corinthians, the apostle Paul said, "After that, in the wisdom of God, the world by wisdom knew not God, it pleased God by the foolishness of preaching to save them that believe. For the Jews require a sign and the Greeks seek after wisdom; but we preach Christ crucified, unto the Jews a stumbling block, and unto the Greeks foolishness; but unto them which are called, both Jews and Greeks, Christ the power of God and the wisdom of God. Because the foolishness of God is wiser than men, and the weakness of God is stronger than men."

In this passage there are three distinct types of character brought into view, which represent very accurately the different classes that have existed in every age under the preaching of the gospel. They are the Jew, the Greek, and the called of God. We have here the formal, superstitious, wonder-loving Jew, accustomed to miracles, and ready to demand a sign from heaven as the only warrant for his faith. We have then the philosophizing, incredulous Greek, scouting every thing as fable and foolishness, which does not answer to his inward sense of beauty and wisdom. And we have also the humble, evangelical believer in Christ, called of God, and taught by the Spirit to put no confidence in Jewish ceremony, or Grecian wisdom, as touching the things of the soul's salvation. Wherever this gospel was proclaimed by Paul and his fellow apostles, most men who heard it long enough to know what it taught, and to be affected by it, might have been ranged into three distinct classes, not inaptly represented by the Jew, the Greek, and the callėd of God. And from that day to this, wherever it has been faithfully preached, these three ancient types have generally reappeared, well defining the positions of all who have heard the gospel, and the feelings with which they have either received or rejected the messages of God. Always and everywhere it has met with the Jew, the Greek, and the humble believer. To some it is still what it was to the self-righteous, ceremonious Jew, a stumbling block. To some it is still just what it was to the self-complacent, boastful Greek, foolishness. While to some, called from the ranks of both Jews and Greeks, it is still all that it was to the primitive disciples, the power of God and the wisdom of God unto salvation.

And thus also, answering to these three classes into which from the beginning the hearers of the gospel have been divided, there have been three widely different and conflicting views of the gospel itself, giving rise to as many different systems within the nominally Christian church, each claiming to be the only true gospel. These are, first, the sacramental system, or formalism, which makes religion consist mainly in externals, the rites and ceremonies of worship, and rigid conformity to ecclesiastical order: secondly, rationalism, or the system which makes human reason the umpire of all revelation, rejecting both mysteries and miracles: and thirdly, the spiritual and evangelical system of grace, whose central truth is Christ crucified as an atoning sacrifice for sin, and which attributes everything good in man to a Divine influence.

Now it is manifest that only the last of these has any claim to be regarded as the true gospel of the New Testament. Ritualism on the one side, and rationalism on the other, are but pretenders, claiming to be a gospel while they are no gospel. And yet many of the creeds and systems that have appeared in the past history of the church, belong to the one error or the other. In all ages men have been found subverting the truth and power of the gospel, by a departure into formalism on the one side or rationalism on the other. And any one, who is himself acquainted with the essential spirit of the gospel, can read the past history of the church, or survey its present condition, and easily assign to its proper place every heresy, and every sect, and every individual opinion. He may classify them with all the exactness of a science. For if not found with Paul, glorying in Jesus Christ and him crucified as the power of God and the wisdom of God unto salvation, they will be found standing in unbelief, with the ceremony-worshipping Jew on the one side, or the reason-worshipping Greek on the other. If Christ Jesus be not exalted to the throne, as all in all, Lord of the conscience, sovereign of the church, and only Saviour of the soul, then either man with his boasting reason, or the church with her ancient prescription, will usurp the throne. The Jew and the Greek are still alive, even among those who call themselves Christians, ever striving to substitute for the true gospel of God that which is another gospel altogether, and is therefore no gospel. The Judaizing teacher of the modern church, forsaking the true faith of the gospel, comes with his venerable traditions and church ceremonies to exalt a ritual service, a baptismal font, a wafer, the pope, or the virgin mother into the place of Christ. The rationalistic teacher on the other hand, in the very spirit of an old Greek, exalts human reason, or art, or man's natural love of the sublime and beautiful, above the very testimony of God's word, and thus baptizing his infidelity with the name of Christian, subverts the gospel of Christ.

It is obvious to remark that the true gospel of Christ, by which he becomes the power of God and the wisdom of God for salvation to all that believe, stands midway between these two extremes, as far removed from the superstitious formalism of the one, as from the sceptical rationalism of the other. The true evangelical system holds this middle position, not because it is any compromise between the antagonistic errors, but because it stood there at the beginning. That is the ancient position. The true gospel was first in the field. And the other systems are but departures from it. Men have undertaken to be wise above what is written, to improve the gospel of God by their philosophies, to devise some more reasonable and acceptable way; and the result in every case has been a departure from the truth, either in the one direction or the other, either in the road which leads through sacramentalism back to Rome, or in the road which leads through rationalism to Pelagianism, Socinianism, infidelity, atheism, and all the modern errors.

The unbelieving Jew of old, and his modern successors, the ritualists and the legalists of every school, unwilling to be saved by Christ alone, and going about to establish their own righteousness, exalt the rites and ceremonies of external worship, and demand conformity, like Nebuchadnezzar, to some great idol image of their own creation; and thus subvert the gospel by vain traditions and legal works. The unbelieving Greek, and his modern successors, the baptized rationalists, and sceptics of every heretical sect, too proud to take the simple story of the cross in its plain and obvious import, rush to the opposite extreme of the scale of error, and discarding not only man's alleged miracles, but God's also, reduce the gospel to a thing of cold, logical reason, until there is nothing Divine left in it, not even the Divinity of Immanuel; and thus subvert the truth by a philosophy, falsely so called. It is not strange, that when men can find no better righteousness than their own to build upon, they should take refuge in the will-worship and superstitions of popery, and kindred forms of sacramentalism. And it is not strange that those who can find in the gospel no trace of Immanuel's Divinity or the Spirit's power, should obey that instinct of the soul which seeks to worship something, and so exalt human reason, or philosophy, or nature, to that throne which Christ ought alone to fill. But it is strange that any human being with the Bible in his hands should so mistake both its letter and its spirit, as to call either the one or the other of these systems the true gospel of God.

To the one class this plain and simple gospel is still a stumbling block, as it was to the Jews at the first; and to the other it is still foolishness, as it was to the Greek. The apostle Paul understood the position of both parties as they stood in his day, and he has virtually anticipated and described the position and character of their successors, down to the present hour. The Jews wanted power—Divine miraculous power that should come down from heaven and consume their enemies. They longed for a temporal kingdom and a visible throne that should dash in pieces all the rulers of thc earth. Their only idea of the Messiah of Israel was that of another David who should treat their enemies as David treated Goliath of Gath. They looked for a deliverer who should come as a conquering king, who should gird on the sword of battle, and adding to all the pomp of earthly grandeur, the supernatural power of Jehovah, should abide for ever, and make Jerusalem at once the terror and the glory of the world. And because Jesus of Nazareth seemed destitute of all these outward signs of power, though claiming to be their Messiah, they rejected his claims and put him to death. The apostle understood precisely their position and their prejudices, for he had once shared in all their ideas and expectations. Brought up at the feet of Gamaliel, a Hebrew of the Hebrews, he well knew the inmost heart of the Jew, that he wanted a religion of miraculous signs, and a Messiah of Divine, irresistible power. And so to the power-loving Jew, who trod the earth with his eye ever fixed upon the heavens for a sign, and whose main objection to the story of the crucified Nazarene, was that it was a gospel of weakness, utter weakness and insufficiency; to him and all like him in every age, Paul replies, We preach a gospel of power, the mighty power of God; we preach a gospel of moral, spiritual, and eternal power; a gospel adequate to do that which all the powers of this world could never do, that is, to secure the pardon of sin and save the soul from death. It is the power of light in a world of darkness; the power of truth in a world of error; the power of holiness in a world of sin; the power of beneficence in a world of selfishness; the power of love in a world of hatred and war; the power of immortality in a world shrouded in death; a gospel bringing the glad tidings from God of pardon, peace, and life from the dead, to souls already sunk in sin, and led captive by the devil at his will. We preach Christ the power of God, unto salvation, for every one that believeth, whether Jew or Greek.

The Greeks, on the other hand, wanted wisdom. They boasted of learning, art, and eloquence. They gloried in philosophy. They longed for some new thing. They had lost the sceptre of military power, and they had exploded the myths and fables, gods and goddesses of their once splendid mythology, the national religion. They had become a nation of reasoners and of sceptics. The highest deity known to their philosophy was human reason, or nature, or man's aesthetic sense of the sublime and beautiful. If there was any higher God in all the Pantheon, he was to them the "unknown God," and belonged solely to another world. Taught by their latest philosophy to regard every thing superhuman as fabulous, they put no confidence in signs and wonders, and were ready to laugh to scorn the first mention of "Jesus and resurrection," as the vain babbling of an impostor. They despised the very things which the Jews most delighted in. They thirsted not for power, but for wisdom; not for old traditions, but for some new thing; not for rites, but for reasons.

The apostle understood their wants precisely; for he was a native of Tarsus, a famous seat of Grecian philosophy. He had doubtless read the books and even attended the schools of this proud, self-complacent race, which regarded all men outside of Greece and her colonies, as barbarians. And thus to the reasoning Greek, seeking after wisdom, and to all like him in every age, who would reject the story of the cross as foolishness, utterly destitute of all philosophy, Paul replies, We preach a gospel of wisdom, the unsearchable wisdom of God; we have not followed cunningly devised fables, the product of a rude and barbarous age, or the device of men aiming to impose upon the world; but we preach that sublime wisdom of God, which none of the princes of this world have ever known, which none of its sages could have discovered, and which, though long hidden from the wise and the prudent, is now revealed in Christ to all the chosen sons of God. We preach Christ the wisdom of God, the true and infallible word of God, able to save unto the uttermost all who come unto God through him, whether Jew or Greek. It is a wisdom which can guide where all other teachers fail; a wisdom which shines brighter and brighter when every light of philosophy goes out in utter darkness. It is a wisdom not limited like the boasted wisdom of the Greeks, to the narrow bounds of that which is but material and perishing, but taking hold of all that is unseen, eternal, Divine. It is the wisdom of the infinite mind—the wisdom of God. It is that wisdom which comes from God, and which alone can raise the soul to God. It is a wisdom adequate to fill all its high and noble faculties both for time and eternity. "In Christ are hid all the treasures of wisdom and knowledge." And well may the apostle exclaim as he surveys all the glorious provisions and promises of such a gospel and such a Saviour, "Oh the depth of the riches, both of the wisdom and knowledge of God!"

To those on the one side therefore who challenge power, clamour for signs and wonders, and are ready to reject the gospel as one of impotence, because it comes not with the insignia of earthly grandeur, Paul proclaims it as the very word of power, sovereign, saving, and eternal power, as much greater than all human power demanded by the Jew, as God is stronger than man. To those on the other side, who clamour for wisdom and make their boast of philosophy, and would reject the gospel as foolishness because it puts no confidence in the flesh, lays the pride of human reason in the dust, and abates not a jot or tittle of its high mysteries to suit the views of men, Paul vindicates it as the only true and saving wisdom in the world, as much greater than all the wisdom conceived of by the Greeks, as God is wiser than men.

It is only because Christ is a Divine Saviour, the power and wisdom of God unto salvation, that the gospel is what it is, the antidote for sin and the hope of a ruined world. This great mystery of godliness is its glory. This has enabled it to stand fast and hold its ground, amid all the errors and conflicts of the eighteen centuries which have passed since its first promulgation at Jerusalem. This has given it power to surmount all opposing forces, the persecutions of its enemies, and the treachery of professing friends, and to press its conquering way from nation to nation, from age to age. Had the gospel been what men have striven so hard to prove it, a mere routine of outward ceremonies on the one hand, or a mere string of abstract propositions commending themselves to human taste on the other, what more could it have done for the world than Jewish tradition or Grecian philosophy did? Had it been nothing more than these it would long ago have perished, even as these have done. But it has had a vitality which earth and hell have not been able to crush; and the secret of this indestructible life is, that it reveals Christ as the power and wisdom of God unto salvation.

And yet, strange to say, though all intelligent readers of the New Testament, who take words in their obvious import, will be ready to acknowledge the justness of this view of the case; still almost every man who hears the story of Christ and him crucified, and does not embrace him with a saving faith, will be found occupying one or the other of these old positions. He either stands where the Jew stood, or where the Greek stood; and it would be difficult to say which side can count the larger number, and which position is the more dangerous. Why does not Christ become a Saviour, believed, accepted, and loved, to that large class of persons in every Christian land, who hear the gospel preached, who read the Scriptures, who assent to the truth, who approve the truth, and even profess to admire it? Why are they still out of Christ? Why are they yet unbelievers as to any real, personal, saving trust in him? They do not intend to live and die without a saving acquaintance with the gospel; and yet they do virtually continue in unbelief, rejecting Christ as their Saviour. For what are such hearers of the gospel waiting? What are they expecting?

If such men will examine their hearts with candour and honesty, they will find that they are either like the Jew, waiting for some more wonderful way, or like the Greek, for some more reasonable way. They are either in the one class or the other, looking for more signs and wonders, before they will believe, or for something in the way of a more convincing logic, in order to make them believe. They have an idea that the fault is not in themselves, but in the gospel; in some want either of supernatural and overpowering attestation before their eyes, or of rational and convincing argument upon their minds.

Some, no doubt, flatter themselves that they will yet be Christians at a more convenient season. But they are waiting for more signal manifestations of God's power. They are not satisfied to take things just as God has revealed them in the gospel, and as thousands of others have had to take them. They demand something peculiar and extraordinary—some dream or vision of the night—something grand and overwhelming. Their case they think is unusual; and it will take something more than common to satisfy their minds. They want a demonstration which is tangible, positive, decisive; which shall flash conviction through the very senses, and put the matter of salvation beyond all question for ever. They would like to have a miracle to make the Bible plainer, and to prove that all the other miracles are from God. They would believe, they think, if one should rise from the dead. They want the kingdom of God to come into their hearts with observation, with somewhat of the same outward pomp and parade with which the Jews wished to see their Messiah come into the world. Like Naaman the Syrian, they think they ought to be healed in a wonderful way; that the prophet ought to come out, and stand before the chariot, and call upon the name of the Lord his God, and strike his hand over the place, and thus recover the leper. In a word, they have the very spirit of the Jew; demanding a sign from heaven, dictating terms to God, and thus seeking to establish their own righteousness. And what does God say to all such? "A wicked and adulterous generation seeketh after a sign, and there shall be no sign given them, save those already given. If they believe not Moses and the prophets, neither will they be persuaded though one rose from the dead. Behold, ye despisers, and wonder and perish. If ye believe not that I am he, ye shall die in your sins."

Some again are standing on the opposite extreme. They desire nothing of this sort. They have no relish for mysteries and marvels in religion. They are not waiting for more signs, but for something to solve the problem of those already given. With them the great difficulty, preventing, as they think, a cordial reception of Christ, is that the gospel is too full of hard sayings, mysterious, incomprehensible doctrines, which do not suit their natural taste, or their logical reason, or their nice, poetic sense of justice, or their admiring perception of the sublime and beautiful. The gospel is not that rational, intelligible, all-merciful, and beautiful system which they think it ought to be. They are doubtful and incredulous as to a thousand difficult points which they would like to have cleared up: and they are waiting for some more reasonable way, or some more convincing argument than they have yet seen, before they can take up the cross and follow Jesus. In short, they are Greeks in spirit; ready to reject the wisdom of God as foolishness, because it is so different from the philosophy of man; and waiting for some new light, and for some auspicious hour, when the skies shall be all clear, and the problems all solved, and the gospel shall become a system level to the calibre of a finite mind! Then they will believe! But that hour will not come, that light will not be given. For this is virtually to reject God's testimony, and to exalt human reason to that throne which belongs to him alone. This is to be wise above what is written in things where none but God can teach man wisdom. And what does Christ say to this self-righteous and exacting spirit which strives for the mastery when it should only believe and adore? "Except ye be converted and become as a little child, ye shall in no wise enter into the kingdom of heaven. If our gospel be hid, it is hid to them that are lost; in whom the god of this world hath blinded the eyes of them which believe not, lest the light of the glorious gospel of Christ, who is the image of God, should shine unto them."

The spirit of the true believer, equally removed from the arrogance of the Jew and the pride of the Greek, is that of a learner and a child, sitting at the feet of Immanuel. Of such is the kingdom of heaven. The true believer takes God's testimony as it is, accredits it as true, the very truth of truth, approves it not only as true, but as right and good, receives and rests upon it as the only and all-sufficient salvation, embraces and glories in Immanuel as the chiefest among ten thousand and altogether lovely, takes up the cross and follows him through evil and through good report, as all in all, for time and for eternity. He asks for no other Saviour; he needs no other; he can depend on no other: he is perfectly satisfied with the gospel as it is; in life, in death, and through eternity, he is willing to fall at Immanuel's feet, to crown him Lord of all, and to cry, as believing Thomas did, "My Lord and my God!"

CHAPTER XIII.

RECAPITULATION AND CONCLUSION.

BUT here we pause; not because we have reached the end, but because what we have said may, at least, suffice to turn the reader's thoughts to that revelation of Immanuel's beauty, which is contained in the sacred word. "His name shall be called Wonderful," said the inspired prophet. His person is wonderful; his character is wonderful; his life and death were wonderful; his work was wonderful; his gospel is wonderful; his first coming was wonderful; his second shall be more so; everything connected with him is wonderful and glorious. It is a boundless theme. It has to man a deathless interest; for it is that which alone brings life and hope to a dying world. In him—in his person, character, and kingdom—are hid all the treasures of wisdom and knowledge. Whatever other treasures of power, wealth, or wisdom, a man may gain, not to know this wisdom is to be a fool indeed, not to gain this unsearchable treasure is to be poor for ever.

And now this gospel of the Son of God, with all its unspeakable blessings, is committed to us, not only to be embraced as our life and the life of our children, but to be made known to the ends of the earth, to be spread abroad to the farthest nations, to be preached to every creature under heaven. "Till I come," is the only termination of the work, the only limit of the great commission. This is the one grand mission and work of the blood-bought church of Christ—to preach his gospel. The field is the world. And the day of labour is from the first to the second advent. He has himself connected these two great events in such a way that the church can never forget the one, or lose sight of the other. "As oft as ye eat this bread and drink this cup, ye do show the Lord's death till he come." Here all that is sacred in the past blends with all that is glorious in the future. We must remember him, must love him, must celebrate his death, must preach his gospel, must labour, and toil, and suffer, and watch, and pray, till he come.

For surely he shall come. As surely as he died and rose again, he shall come. Now we see through a glass darkly. Now we know in part and we understand in part. But then we shall see face to face, and know even as we are known. We know not yet what we shall be; but we know that when he shall appear we shall be like him. Our vile bodies shall be fashioned like unto his glorious body. Our life is hid with Christ in God, so that when he shall appear, we shall appear with him in glory. This is our hope, this our confident and joyful expectation. "To you," says the apostle, "who are troubled, rest with us in hope, when the Lord Jesus shall be revealed from heaven, with his mighty angels, in flaming fire, taking vengeance on them that know not God, and that obey not the gospel of our Lord Jesus Christ; who shall be punished with everlasting destruction from the presence of the Lord, and from the glory of his power; when he shall come to be glorified in his saints, and to be admired in all them that believe."

In the person and character of Immanuel, we are to remember, God has made the brightest manifestation of himself. "No man hath seen God at any time; the only begotten Son who is in the bosom of the Father, he hath declared him." "He that hath seen me," said Jesus, "hath seen the Father." We know the heart of God even as we know the heart of Jesus. We become acquainted with the character of God, as we become personally acquainted with the character of Jesus. "For God who commanded the light to shine out of darkness, hath shined in our hearts, to give the light of the knowledge of the glory of God in the face of Jesus Christ." There are various methods in which God has manifested his character and glory to his intelligent, moral creatures; and there are manifold channels through which this glory shines. He has revealed himself everywhere in nature, every work of his almighty hand proclaiming his glory. He has revealed himself in providence, every event, great and small, uttering an intelligible voice. He has revealed himself in every page of his written and inspired oracles—the holy Scriptures. He has revealed himself also in the work of the Holy Ghost upon the regenerated human soul; and, indeed, in all the deep instincts and utterances of the soul itself. But, above all other manifestations is this glorious manifestation of the word made flesh. For here it is that we behold the essence of all Divine knowledge and perfection—infinite wisdom, goodness, truth, beauty, and love, personified, embodied, exemplified in the character of a living man like ourselves, in all points tempted as we are, yet without sin. This is the manifestation of God which comes nearest to our bosoms, and is most easily understood by us.

We learn something of God in every manifestation he has made of himself. Day unto day uttereth speech of him; night unto night showeth knowledge. There is no speech nor language where his voice is not heard. The signs of his eternal power and Godhead overspread the heavens. His glory fills the earth. His stately steppings are seen in the great waters. His wisdom shines in every star that gems the firmament. His mighty acts are visible in all the movements of his providence. His justice, holiness, and truth are proclaimed from every line of his word. The thunders of his law, the beseeching overtures of his gospel, the gentle, yet irresistible, pleadings of his gracious Spirit—all alike make known to man something of the deep things of God. But it is in Immanuel, most of all, that the soul of man finds the clear light of God. He above all others is the way, and the truth, and the life.

"Till God in human flesh I see,
My thoughts no comfort find;
The holy, just, and sacred Three
Are terrors to my mind.
But if Immanuel's face appear
My hope, my joy begins;
His name forbids my slavish fear,
His grace removes my sins."

Ten thousand times ten thousand guilty, helpless, dying sinners in all ages, have been led to admire the beauty of Immanuel, as they have seen him to be the only and all-sufficient Saviour, both able and willing to give them that succour which no other being in the universe could ever give. As they have found in him a friend and a helper just suited to their lost estate—the sacrifice for all their sins, the supply of all their wants, the antidote to all their woes, the Prophet, Priest, King, and Captain of their salvation, they have been made to rejoice with a joy unspeakable and full of glory. For all the manifestations of God's character, however made, and for all the gifts of his grace, however communicated, we ought to be profoundly grateful. But for the gift of his Son—for the manifestation of his amazing love in Christ, how can we ever sufficiently praise him! Where shall we find words to express, or images to shadow forth, our conception of the debt of gratitude which we owe to God for such a Saviour! We can only take the language of an apostle and cry—"Thanks be unto God for his unspeakable gift."

When we consider what Jesus hath done for us—how he left the bright abodes of glory and stooped to our lost estate—how he hath borne our griefs and carried our sorrows in his own body on the tree—how he endured all that men and demons could inflict while drinking for us the wrath of God—how he hath taken our feet from an horrible pit and from the miry clay, and placed them upon the rock of ages, and put a new song into our mouths, even the song of praise for his delivering grace—how he hath made us, who were by nature the children of wrath and heirs of death, the children of adoption, sons and daughters of the Lord Almighty, heirs of God, and joint heirs with himself to an inheritance which is incorruptible, undefiled, and that fadeth not away, reserved in heaven for all them that believe, we can only fall in adoring homage at his feet, and cry, "Thanks be to God for his unspeakable gift."

When we think of life here, as it is to some, and as it would be to us, without him—the loneliness, desolation, and darkness of a life without hope and without God in the world; when we think how we should feel and act, with every light of the gospel and every hope of heaven for ever extinguished in our souls; when the friends of our youth have all fallen around us; when the dearest objects of our human affections are sleeping in the ground; when all our bodily powers give token of approaching decay and dissolution, and the storms of adversity are beating upon our souls; when our days are all sunless, and our nights without a star, and there seems nothing before us but the blackness of death —unending death—Oh! when we think of such a condition as this—the condition of the unbelieving sceptic, who cares nothing for Jesus, and then think of all that he has done for us, and of the glory which yet awaits us, we cry with adoring and admiring homage, "Thanks be to God for his unspeakable gift!"

When, as God's suffering children, we pass through many a dark valley of humiliation on life's weary pilgrimage; when we are compelled to eat the bread of carefulness, to drink the cup of tears, to wrestle with gloomy doubts and fears, to feel that the deep waters are ready to engulf us; when all our plans of life seem to fail, our best purposes to be defeated, our fondest hopes to be utterly crushed and blasted; when all our enemies have risen up against us; when the world has cheated us, friends and kindred have forsaken us, and the very church and people of God deceived us; when our very heart-strings are breaking for sorrow, and there seems nothing left for us but to lie down and die—wretched, poor, despised, forsaken, tired of the world, and yet feeling unfit for heaven—counting all men liars, and yet unable to look up lovingly and confidingly into the face of God—Oh! in such an hour of temptation and despondency, what a voice of consolation is that which comes to us from the lips of Jesus, as we open again the sacred pages, and, with streaming eyes, read those calm, tender, soul-subduing, and unfathomable words, "Ye believe in God; believe also in me! In my Father's house are many mansions; if it were not so, I would have told you; I go to prepare a place for you. And if I go and prepare a place for you, I will come again, and receive you unto myself, that where I am there ye may be also." And then, if never before, we cry, with chastened, humble, loving hearts, "Thanks be unto God for his unspeakable gift!"

"For such compassions, O my God,
Ten thousand thanks are due—
For such compassions, I esteem
Ten thousand thanks too few."

And when, at last, we look forward to the time of our departure from this mortal scene, and are called to pass through the dark valley and shadow of death; when our earthly house of this tabernacle is about to be dissolved, and we feel that with every heaving breath and every ebbing pulse we are but drawing nearer and nearer to the presence of God; when we feel that in the lone and untried valley we need a guide and a comforter, a rod and a staff to support our trembling footsteps, a friendly bosom on which to lean the weary head, an Almighty arm to protect us, and a voice of love to cheer us and bid us fear no evil—where then shall we find the guide and comforter of our souls? Who but Immanuel can be with us then, go with us through all the darkness of death, and bid us welcome to the fields of immortality, when it is passed? When we feel, as we must all soon feel, that the only guide and counsellor through this dread passage, is Jesus; that the only rod and staff to comfort us there, the only loving bosom on which we can lean our dying heads, and the only friendly voice which can come to cheer us, is that of Jesus who hath trodden it before us, well may we cry, "Thanks be to God!—Glory be to God in the highest for this unspeakable gift! Blessed be the God and Father of our Lord Jesus Christ, who, according to his abundant mercy, hath begotten us again to a lively hope, by the resurrection of Jesus Christ from the dead."

God with us! God incarnate! God our Saviour, Brother, Lord! How it should elevate our thoughts, how it should kindle our devotions, how it should bind our hearts in holy love to contemplate the great and blessed mystery of God manifest in the flesh! that God has been with us, and that we shall be with him for ever, he in our nature, and we through him made partakers of the Divine nature! What more could God do for us? What more do we need in order that Christ should win our hearts?

When we think of the loved ones, who were so recently with us, who have left the church below and gone up to the general assembly and church of the first-born, having washed their robes and made them white in the blood of the Lamb—when we look around upon our broken family circles, and feel that those with whom we took sweet counsel here, are now in the presence of Jesus, beholding his glory face to face—when we think of all those venerable and honoured names, whose praises were in all the church below, and whose toil-worn but happy spirits have passed away, even during the last year, to join the ranks and to swell the chorus of the redeemed on high—when we think that these with the saints of all ages are now with Jesus, and that we also, after a few more years of toil and sorrow, shall join their blessed company, to part no more for ever; how should our hearts burn within us, as we tell of Immanuel's love, of all that we owe to him, and of all that we hope to be!

Here then let us come, even to the cross of Immanuel; here let us find rest in a sense of his love; here let us admire and adore, as, for time and eternity, we commit our souls to his keeping.

www.ingramcontent.com/pod-product-compliance
Lightning Source LLC
LaVergne TN
LVHW011215110826
845150LV00006B/1435